Defining Modern Day Black Momma®

Who Is She?

Now, Her Future and

Who She Should Never Become:

A Self-Love Essay

Written

by

Felice Bois

Library of Congress Control Number: 2021916570

ISBN: 978-0-578-96842-1 (Paperback)

Legal Disclaimer: Felice Bois is a creative writer. This is a work of creative non-fiction. The information contained in this essay is subject to change with or without notice.

All events in this essay are true to the best of the author's memory or the product of the author's imagination or used in a fictitious manner. Some names, characters, businesses, places, events, incidents and identifying features have been changed to protect the identity of certain parties.

This essay represents the personal views and opinions of the author and does not necessarily reflect the positions or opinions of any organization, institution, or individual with which the author is affiliated. The content presented herein is based on the author's perspective and interpretation of the subject matter. Neither the publisher nor any associated parties shall be held responsible for any consequence arising from the opinions or interpretations expressed within this essay.

Be sure to talk to your physician, spouse and/or loved ones before making life altering changes. The author's life experiences, facts, philosophy and personal opinions shared in this essay is not intended as medical or legal advice and may not be applicable for everyone.

Contents

Preface

This self-love essay has allowed me to weave together fabrics of the life of my past, who I am now and my future. It is my warmest wish that this self-love essay will encourage other Black women to begin weaving in the fabrics of everything (words, actions of others, etc.) that defined her past, her present life now, and her altered future of [becoming] to breathe life into an honest meaningful new narrative of herself.

I wrote this self-love essay to restore my heart, my dignity and to bring a broader, meaningful definition to my life and my brand – Modern Day Black Momma® - in retrospect, has had an inconclusive definition since the inception of the poem Modern Day Black Momma® in 2006, the first copyright in 2008 and a subsequent copyright and CD publication in 2009 and finally this essay.

In the early 2000s, my heart had been broken, I was suffering for over two decades as of this writing, excluding the traumatic events I experienced as a child and in my teenage years. Prior to the last twenty years, I had experienced living as young ambitious Black woman, a mother and a single parent working in public service providing administrative services to large corporations and non-profit agencies within Northern California while also working as a licensed real estate agent. During that time, I hadn't reached my full financial potential, and yet, I was striving for excellence while raising my two children: one male pre-teen and a young daughter under the age of five – we were surviving and paying the bills but not thriving.

We were a struggling African American family living from paycheck to paycheck. In addition to that, I had to deal with the complexities of motherhood – raising a young African American teenage son, whom I love dearly – he was my first inspiration and motivation to live and embrace the world even though as a teenage mother then, I couldn't fathom what fierceness the world would bring to us in the future. Then the economic downturn in 2007– the California recession hit, the real estate market collapsed – I was laid off work, could barely afford rent or to pay for our groceries – we were living on our last dollar – marching like a colony of ants with thousands of other families right into the welfare line.

All my hard work for my family was shattering – everything I was building for us had fallen into pieces – I was sick all the time – for years, I was so sick that I my only outlet to release the emotional pain was to write. Life said, "write", and that's what I did - all I did was write. Anything and everything my brain needed to say, I scribbled it, scratched it, threw it away, started over, typed it or wrote it again. Writing medicated the neurological shock that impacted my brain – so writing poetry and stage plays creatively became my medicine to bring me some calmness because my voice was fighting to get out of me all the time. I experienced constant epiphanies – philosophical and prolific moments that I could not hold inside my mind – eventually, I embarked into the literary world as unknown and unpublished creative writer/artist. I have stacks of literary works I haven't published yet. Writing poetry became the voice on paper that I never knew – I didn't know that I could write in that depth. Then one day, I decided to record my poetry as spoken word because my spirit was constantly inclined to be
outwardly vocal– the sounds, the vibrations and rhythms of music was always a presence in my ear – I could hear music that I never heard before – I saw images I had to write about – and if I

didn't respond to my epiphanies by writing, I could've succumbed to my broken heart. I wanted to live, which is why I write in the capacity that I do, when I have to because the words touch something in my brain that temporarily filters out some of the pain in my heavy heart. In retrospect, writing poetry, stage plays, and other creative writing, helped me to survive in my brokenness and to potentially help others who have fallen through the cracks hear my voice so they would know they are not alone in their pain and suffering.

Inspired by my creativity in combination with my imagination and real-life past experiences, I started my own small publishing company Modern Day Black Momma® Records, and published my first sound recording – Gen Eyes Wide, first released in May 2009. It was published on most social media musical platforms such as Facebook, Tiktok, Spotify, Amazon and Youtube. But it was the musical platform Reverbnation.com/felicebois that developed most of my fanbase and reviews for the Gen Eyes Wide album – where sincere heartfelt comments are always posted. And, as I grew to learn that the spirit and lyrics of my spoken word had encouraged and inspired hope or triggered positive memories in the lives of my listeners – over a span of years, I continued to write while still in great emotional pain.

To add to my brokenness, I was being robbed of my intellectual property Gen Eyes Wide which featured the poem "Modern Day Black Momma®". A well-known Hollywood movie producer writer/director who I believe had access to the poem used my characters to help build his movie manuscript which was written, copywritten and published within a year after I published Gen Eyes Wide. When I saw my poem being acted out on screen with these famous actresses combined with another poet/writer's work, from another era, with no attribution to my name – I was devasted and heart-broken – again. I remember reading the credits at the end of the movie a dozen times – over a span of years, my name Felice Bois wasn't there; no letter in the mail, no check in my bank account – nothing but silence, stillness and anger had overcome me. I've felt furious and helpless for years.

Then, there I was – living under a pile of rocks, nobody could see [me]. I was not well known in the literary or entertainment world – how could I go up against this conglomerate of a phenomenon's lawyers and not look like a gold digger? My heart has been lost for words ever since for fourteen whole years. After the movie was published, and after careful examination of the other poet's literary works – I discovered, there were no similarities in our literary work with the exception that we talk about the condition of African American women but different issues in a different era of time – different styles of poetry. The movie producer combined both of our literary works, but in my opinion, my poem is carrying the majority of the movie – similar to the work of a supporting actress. The movie is his adaptation, and his dialogue but inspired by our poems, the condition of the Black woman, to build his characters in the script. Without our poems, he wouldn't have written the script or published the movie. I've counted frame by frame of the movie which documents that the poem Modern Day Black Momma® exist in his movie.

If you've ever watched a movie that closely describes my characters as described in the poem Modern Day Black Momma®, just remember I AM the original writer and rightful owner.

I have never met this famous movie producer personally and I don't know anyone who knows him. So why would a wealthy movie producer use my literary work, as his own, to write a screenplay and publish it as a movie film? Timing – good timing. It was good timing to publish a movie surrounding the topics and issues of African American women in Black America. My beliefs are that he learned about my poem Modern Day Black Momma® through the grapevine – "word of mouth" because it travels fast. The acapella poem was available for online streaming, online single downloads or to purchase the physical CD from CDBaby which I had numerous anonymous orders. I might add, that the movie producer is a very talented writer, producer, director, actor – and I don't hate him; however, this type of behavior is called – plagiarism.

He may have attempted to contact me or maybe he never had intentions to ever contact me because my name at the time was attached to negative media. In my personal opinion, he didn't want my name attached to his new stardom and again, I was not a well-known artist or writer – I was a new self-published spoken word artist. The problem with this subject matter sitting in my heart all these years, is that he used too much of my literary work to make the movie. He created the dialogue for the characters, but used the other writer's work as the theme to create his hit movie – and millions of dollars were made using [our] poetry.

This is why branding Modern Day Black Momma® is so important, so important that someone of his stature would use my literary work in his movie in the same way I would have used it if I had the monetary resources and access to actors to help bring the poem into reality. Eventually, I wrote the stage play Modern Day Black Momma® to regain some recourse to help rebuild my confidence and continuity in my life journey. My self-dignity was damaged because of the robbing and illegal use of my literary works without my permission. I was already heart broken and as of this present day, I have not been contacted by the famous movie producer.

For Black women all over the world – our stories not only add value and clarity, a close-up view into the condition of our lives but we add rich history to Black Art. Black women such as Phillis Wheatly (Poet/Author), sold into slavery as a small child – first African American to publish a book in the United States of America – an African American woman who forged a fork in African American literary and intellectual works since 1767. Then new generations of women such as Maya Angelou (Poet/Author, Civil Rights Activist), Shirley Chisholm (Former Congresswoman/Author), Toni Morrison (Author/Editor), Oprah Winfrey (Host/Television Producer), Terry McMillan (Novelist/Producer/Screenwriter), Michelle Obama (Former First Lady of the USA/Author), Shonda Rhymes (Producer/Screenwriter), Kamala Harris (Vice President of the USA/Author) – just to name a few female creatives – our stories sale and are relevant because although some might see the African American culture or our social status as undignified or irrelevant, we are a present force with an aptitude to be reckoned with – our ambitions, our talents, the worthiness of our imagination, our relevance in American history – the respect of our life journeys must be acknowledged.

Black women should always control our own life narratives even if someone attempts to steal our story and make it their own in this lifetime or in our death, but you know what? One day – my God, my Lord, the roaring of his shores, and the thunders of his lightening will come a knockin'.

iv.

Dedication

This Essay is Dedicated to Myself, first.

Although, I was living, I didn't understand this life, what I was living for or the consequences of living in the strength of my own free will, aimlessly in my youthful years, within a world where I was forced to learn to live, survive, thrive and maintain a crown that I did not see.

~Felice Bois

Time to Heal

To my sweet daughter CoraMay and for every Black woman who somehow got stuck in the cracks that squeezed the life out of your journey, the strength you need lies in the power of your intelligence and God almighty.

"A time to heal; a time to break down, and a time to build up; a time to weep, and a time to dance." Ecclesiastes 3:1 (KJV).

The Origin of the Modern Day Black Momma®

African American women (nurses, maids, or missionaries). Picture taken during or after the abolishment of American slavery.

The origin of the Modern Day Black Momma® predates the European colonization era, before the Trans-Atlantic Slave Trade began during 1619-1865. Historically, Black people were identified racially as a Kushi (Hebrew: dark skinned person), African, Black, Mulatto, Colored, Negro, and African Americans. Today, separate from the Black male, Black women are also known as a Modern Day Black Momma® - a neology, a formal phrase that collectively and racially identifies Black women – collectively because people of color have seven or more identifying racial categories as I have previously identified.

Kidnapping and enslaving African women as economic commodities were common improprieties first documented in the *Dead Sea Scrolls* (original Old Testament bible) which was later translated from its original Hebrew, Aramaic, Greek languages and published in the King James Version (KJV) bible which also includes the New Testament of the Gospel of Jesus Christ.

Dead Sea Scrolls

However, there were many versions of the Holy Bible published before the King James Version; I personally agree that the King James Version is closest to the original text of the Dead Sea Scrolls (original Old Testament) because it is not a human influenced doctrine of theology. It is the true God (creator of the human race), inspired doctrine.

1

The Modern Day Black Momma® (Black women or women of color) has always existed but the actual usage or neology — the phrase Modern Day Black Momma® was not formally penned or introduced to the public until I first redefined Black women when I first wrote the poem *Modern Day Black Momma®* in 2006, then self-published it in May 2009. The poem is included with a collection of seventeen acapella prose poems on the Gen Eyes Wide compact disc album — recorded, then published in audio format. Until the publishing of this essay, the formal definition of Modern Day Black Momma® was inconclusive.

As a creative writer, author and recording artist, I have a literary catalog of unpublished and published poems and songs, including two unpublished stage plays: "Modern Day Black Momma®" and "Who You Gon' Be" catalogued at the United States Copyright Office.

The Modern Day Black Momma® Movement

The Modern Day Black Momma® movement originated after the

first indigenous African female chattel slave was kidnapped, sold, or given as a gift before or during the European colonization era, as a result, exasperated a systemic global struggle for meaningful equality for Black women who are highly driven career professionals, mothers, grandmothers, wives, sisters and aunts who still widely suffer from historical ongoing injustices - a constant struggle to rise above the status quo. Hence, an ongoing emergence of African descendants of formerly enslaved indigenous female Africans who continue to grapple through the disenfranchisement of the Modern Day Black Momma® and the African American family.

The Definition

Modern Day Black Momma®

Noun. madən/ˈdeɪ /ˈblæk/ˈmamə (U.S. English Phonetic Pronunciation)

1. Any indigenous African female chattel slave who was kidnapped, sold or given as a gift and forced into chattel slavery before or during the European colonization era.

2. A free displaced African/Black female *descendant* (in the African Diaspora) of an indigenous African chattel slave, who was kidnapped, sold or given as a gift and forced into chattel slavery before or during the European colonization era. (*e.g., Black women within the African Diaspora who have been displaced outside of the continent of Africa. Or, African American women displaced from their indigenous homeland of Africa and forced to live in different geographical locations throughout the world and are no longer subjected or controlled through chattel slavery.*)

3. A Black woman or a group of Black women in any part of the geographical world.

4. African Diaspora. African people who were involuntarily dispersed or spread throughout the world in the British Colonies of North America, New England and the Western United States of America from their original homeland of Africa.

Adjective

1. The Modern Day Black Momma® *(Black women)* was oppressed and enslaved for more than 246 years, (during European colonization and African slavery, [1619-1865]), during the official Black Codes and Jim Crow laws, and after segregation legally ended, [1865-1954], leading up to mass incarceration of African Americans in the early 1970s-present.

2. It is my personal opinion that the Modern Day Black Momma® *(Black women)* suffer from disturbing higher rates of Post-Traumatic Stress Disorder (PTSD) than white women.

Adjective Expanded for Clarification

Indigenous kidnapped and enslaved African women before or during the European colonization era, (also known as a Modern Day Black Momma® in the 21ˢᵗ century) were stripped from their homeland and forced to settle, integrate, and provide free labor to their slave owners.

Subsequently, enslaved African women were demonized, beaten and controlled intellectually. They were sexualized and raped, as a result, physical and mental illnesses paired with infant mortality rates, which were high among enslaved African women, where most infants died within their first year of birth. But surviving child births of enslaved African women continued to increase in size throughout America and other countries, forming a new population of chattel slaves in unfamiliar geographical continents, such as Europe, South America, North America and Asia; therefore, creating a generational modern Creole culture of mixed races, languages, religious beliefs, arts, and oppressive democracies.

Inevitably, causing a diaspora of displaced generational Black descendants dispersed throughout the world, subjected to dehumanization, and systemic racism. Hence, a denial and persistent fight for equal rights in housing, education, medical care, career and wealth building opportunities, unlawful and unwarranted mass incarcerations resulting in deplorable numbers of absentee fathers, unwed mothers and single parent households. Therefore, depleting the African American family structure and value of what the African American family was meant to be, at the same time, increasing crime rates in low income and poverty infested communities.

Further Definitions of Modern Day Black Momma®

Mother of Light - Before God breathed air into man, He first separated the darkness from the light because each entity serves its own purpose within the universe. In darkness, there is life, power and strength; however, life in darkness survives in great difficulty or it suffers and dies. In addition, light, generates life, power and strength, too, but it also reveals *all truth*; and as long as there is light, then there is life and It Isn't as dim as it is in darkness.

As a mother of light, always separate yourselves from the darkness so that your wisdom, life and energy will bring light into the darkness around you. You are a relevant woman, wherever you are in the world, because God created you to give life and to pursue it and thrive.

Modern - As women we must always reinvent ourselves, renew our minds, our spirits, to not only survive and thrive, but for the *purpose* of our lives to become fruition. We must keep up with *time* and *waste* none of it, and use your God given gifts and talents purposefully and wisely.

Day - God gave us light so we can see. Our time on earth is limited to what we can accomplish while living as long as we have *light* and *time*.

Black - God gave the color *Black* - life. All shades of Black are beautiful. Black is not darkness. Black is not colorless because we can see it. Black people were meant to be seen. And, although some people may see the diversity in the color of our skin tones as a challenge to their psychological darkness, God will give them light when it's time for them to see. God is the light that gives us life in our Blackness.

Momma vs. Mama - Both words "momma" and "mama" are used interchangeably and universally when children refer to a woman whom is their mother; at the same time, the mother becomes the matriarch of her family whether she is married or a single parent.

Mother - Women were created originally to be a helpmeet to a man – to serve as a wife or companion. In addition, women were born with a substantial number of eggs in the female reproductive system to procreate with a man and give life to humanity. Women were born to create life, be wives to their husbands, mother their children, give hope to the motherless and use our innate gifted abilities in any other areas that life demands. As mothers we protect what we love. We fight for love and to be loved. Women learn to nurture love. We are natural warriors, protectors, and healers. The touch of a loving mother is priceless. She can help heal a broken soul and heal psychological wounds through words of wisdom from God.

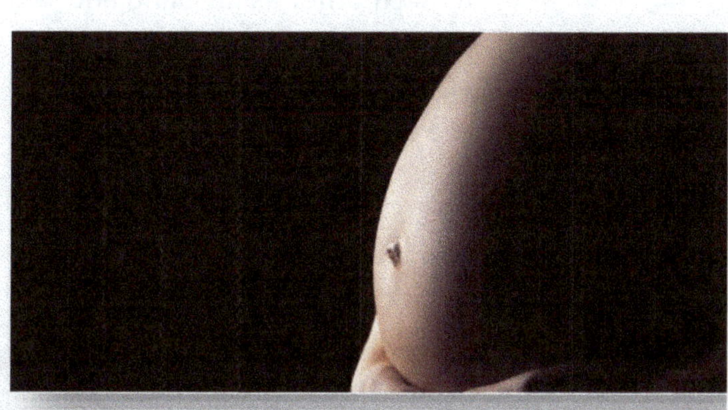

Born to Be Mothers

Biologically, the DNA of a *woman* was derived from the first human man created by God in the history of the human race – his given name was Adam (Greek, [*of the ground or taken out of the red earth]*) Adham, [Hebrew]. The spiritual DNA of every woman is derived from God. God is a spirit and his Son Jesus Christ (John 4:24, *"The firstborn of every creature"*, Col. 1:15-19, *[KJV].*) "In the beginning, the *Word* (*Jesus Christ*) was with God, and the *Word* was God", (John 1:1, 1 John 1:1). Together, they are the creators of the universe, of all living things, and the DNA of which all humanity has derived, (Genesis 1.1, Colossians 1:16, John 5:7, Psalms 102:25, Hebrews 1:10, John 1:3, 17:5, KJV). The Holy Bible (KJV) says in Genesis 1:27 *"God created man in his own image, in the image of God created he him; male and female created he them."*

In Genesis 2:7 the bible says *"the Lord God formed man of the dust of the ground, breathed into his nostrils the breath of life; and the man became a living soul"* then he put the man Eastward

in the Garden of Eden (*Genesis* 2:8). There, he gave Adam instructions on how to care for the Garden of Eden and simultaneously saw that Adam was alone and didn't have a companion, which is why God caused Adam to fall into a deep sleep and "took one of his ribs" (Adam), (Genesis 2:21), and created a woman with his rib and brought her to Adam who then said – *"This is now bone of my bones, and flesh of my flesh; she shall be called Woman, because she was taken out of man,"* (Genesis 2:23); which means, God, Jesus Christ and Adam are Eve's ancestors.

Adam and Eve's marriage was the first and official, spiritual, monogamous, romantic wedding ceremony on earth designed to last a lifetime. The wedding begins, first, with the creation of the woman; second, God brought her to Adam; thirdly, Adam accepts his gift of the woman from God; and fourthly, Adam confesses who the woman will be to him.

The monogamy of the marriage (*e.g.*, their connection and loyalty to each other as husband and wife, as life partners) begins when God created Eve for Adam from his rib; second, when Adam spoke his vows to Eve, saying: "bones of my bones, flesh of my flesh" – the marriage became monogamous. God created the marriage for the husband to have one wife and the wife to have one husband. Eve belongs to Adam and he belongs to Eve.

Adam's wedding vows to Eve permeated emotions of love and care; adding to that – his vows weaved in a form of excitement and mystery revealing a love connection between a husband and wife. His spiritual vows to her are beautiful! Kinda reminds me of that famous nightclub scene with Diana Ross and Billy Dee Williams in the 1972 melodrama movie, "Lady Sings the Blues". While sitting in the audience unbeknownst to Diana Ross's character, (Billie Holiday) who's shyly singing to her audience – suddenly looks to her left, and this handsome, charming Black man, Billy Dee Williams' character, (Louis McKay) – whose hair was styled in shiny black finger waves – he was elegantly dressed in a pin stripped black suit. He then slowly emerges out of the shadows of his seat into the show lights, with his hand reaching out to her offering Billy Holiday a fifty-dollar tip. Girl! – you know the rest – his arm did not fall off. Although, they had a love-hate friendship and marriage, it is my opinion, the next best thing a Black woman could have back then in the 70s, or at any time, since the evolution of human existence – is the love of a husband.

Adam, however, was the first and original romantic king. He was wise enough to accept the gift of the woman God had given him and embraced her immediately. Adam was Eve's king in the earth. The bible says: "Whoso findeth a wife, findeth a good thing, and obtaineth favour of the Lord," (Proverbs 18:22, KJV).

Anywho…It is my perspective that Adam's rib symbolizes "protection" and "covering" over Eve and their children because the ribs from the rib cage of the human body protects human organs, such as the lungs and the heart. He is her protector and leader because she is the "weaker vessel" and "it was Adam who was first created – then Eve," and "for the husband is the head of the wife" (Ephesians 5:23-29, John 10:1, 1 Peter 3:7, 1 Timothy 2:13-14). When Adam says "This is now bone of my bones, and Flesh of my flesh" that was his vow of fidelity (loyalty and faithfulness) to his wife Eve because she was created for him as his helpmeet – to be a helpful companion in the earth.

Although the original name given to *Eve* by her husband was *Woman, (Genesis 2:23)* it wasn't until after their fall from God's grace that Adam called his wife *Eve* the *"mother of all living"* (Genesis 3:20). Eve (Hebrew; Hawwah, life, living) and in Modern Western Culture Christianity, *Eve* is known as the *Mother of the Human Race, Mother of Life* or the *Mitochondrial Eve* - The mitochondrial DNA (*mtDNA*) of *Eve*

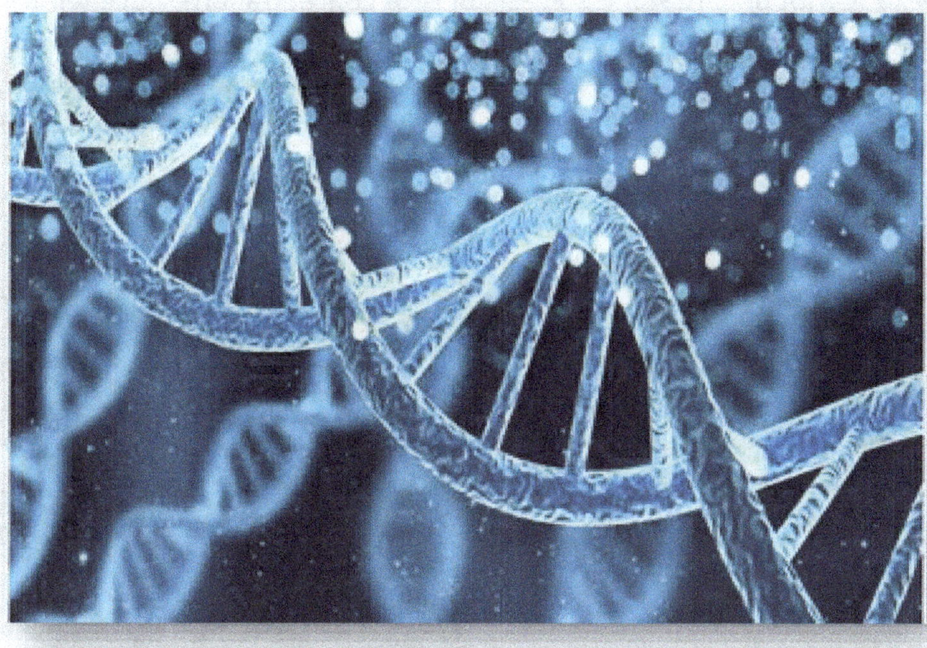

traces all ancestral human life back to the continent of Africa. According to a 1991 publication published by UC Berkeley's Media Relations department, it was through the studies of molecular evolution, Alan C. Wilson, a scientist and UC Berkeley professor of biochemistry and molecular biology revealed the following DNA discovery during his scientific research:

"For the past 10 years he and his colleagues have concentrated on DNA in the mitochondria, an energy-producing organ inside every cell that contains its own complement of genes separate from the genes in the nucleus of the cell. These mitochondrial genes are inherited only from the mother.

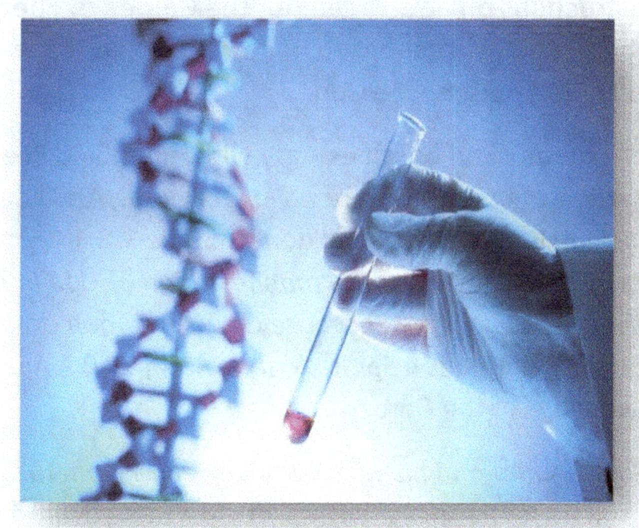

Based on an analysis of mitochondrial DNA from people of various races, he and his colleagues in 1987 hypothesized that all humans living today have mitochondria traceable to a common ancestor who lived around 200,000 years ago in an African population.

The actual existence of Eve, "the mother of us all," is still a topic of debate among scientists."
(Shared with permission. UC Berkley.)
https://newsarchive.berkeley.edu/news/media/releases/archival/allan_wilson_obit.shtml).

Yes, scientists were able to prove what God had already revealed generation through generation – took a lot of hard work, 10 years of DNA concentration – but their hard work prevailed.

As I mentioned earlier, Eve was created by God in the Garden of Eden after God created the first human man, her husband, Adam. Before God created Adam and Eve, he created the *universe* from darkness – The bible says *"the earth was <u>without form</u>, and <u>void</u>; and <u>darkness</u> was upon the face of the deep"* (Genesis 1:1-5). The sky (firmament) didn't even exist yet, can you imagine that?

Prior to God creating the woman from Adam's rib, God had already given Adam instructions on how to care for the Garden of Eden; consequently, Adam and Eve both failed to obey God's instructions to not eat from the Tree of Knowledge of Good and Evil (Genesis 2:17, KJV). They disobeyed God.

As a result, God became angry with Adam and Eve because he knew they both sinned in the Garden of Eden and were *no longer pure.* And when they heard the voice of the Lord God walking in the Garden of Eden (Genesis 3:8, KJV), they could see the Lord God in theophany form, (*the appearance or manifestation of God in human form, although God was not in physical human form because God is not man or look like a man because He is a spirit*). The bible says *"God is a Spirit…"* (John 4:24, KJV) – Adam and Eve both heard the voice of God *"walking"* in the Garden.

Then *"Adam and his wife hid themselves from the presence of God"* (Genesis 3:8, KJV); they were no longer physically naked, instead, covered with aprons made of fig leaves, impure and ashamed of their sinful behavior. Adam was afraid to face God because he didn't obey God and failed to follow the instructions (*Adam knew God could see his sin, his nakedness*) that God had given him in the Garden of Eden (Genesis 3:10, KJV), to not eat from the Tree of Knowledge of Good and Evil.

The serpent (Satan) convinced Eve to ignore Gods [will], his life instructions, instead, deceived Eve into believing that God was hiding something from her and Adam. First, the serpent convinced Eve by saying: *"Ye shall not surely die"* (Genesis 3:3, KJV), and furthermore, convinced Eve, they would *"be as gods knowing good and evil,"* (Genesis 3:5, KJV). Furthermore, Genesis 3:6-7, KJV) says Eve saw *"the tree was good for food,* and that it was *'pleasant'* to the eyes." Eve also believed the tree could make them

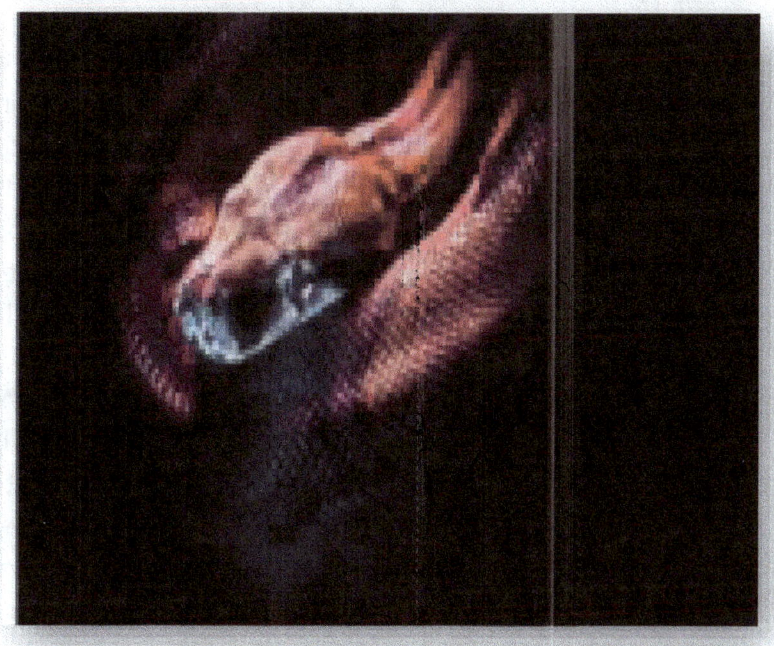

"wise", therefore, Eve ate the fruit, and then Adam ate the fruit (Genesis 3:6, KJV).

The serpent deceived Eve into believing that if she ate the fruit from the Tree of Knowledge of Good and Evil, their eyes would be open and would *"make one wise"* (Genesis 3:6 KJV), instead, their eyes were opened to their nakedness – their *sin* separated them from the [will] and presence of God (Genesis 3:7, KJV).

God's desire and choice for Adam and Eve's life in the Garden of Eden was diminished by their disobedience. Both their lives spiraled into the inevitable life of impurity and spiritual darkness.

God judged and cursed Adam and Eve. He said to Eve *"I will greatly multiply thy sorrow and <u>thy conception; in sorrow thou shalt bring forth children</u>..."* (Genesis 3:16, KJV). At the same time God told Adam *"cursed is the ground for thy sake; in sorrow shalt thou eat of it all the days of thy life; ...for out of it wast thou taken: for dust thou art, and onto dust shalt thou return"* (Genesis 3:17-19, KJV).

After God cursed Adam and Eve, He *"drove out man"* and sealed the Garden of Eden with *"Cherubims and a flaming sword which turned every way, to keep the way of the Tree of Life"* (Genesis 3:24, KJV).

Adam and Eve became wanderers in a strange land here on earth, somewhere east of Eden. Then, Adam called his wife's name Eve because she was the *"mother of all living"* (Genesis 3:20, KJV). In that moment, I believe Adam and Eve knew they would inherently become procreators of new human life in a wandering world of good and evil with indefinite sorrows for many generations to come.

After the manifestation of their fall from grace, a spiritual world war between God and the beast (man's sinful and evil nature) continues throughout the world as human beings fight for

liberty from the destruction of ourselves, for the duration of humanity on earth because the woman and the man in the Garden of Eden didn't choose the Tree of Life. Consequently, every time a baby girl is born, a mother is born with the burdens of questionable futures for every infant child born of *free-will* into a sinful nature (the liberty to choose between right and wrong [to sin or not sin] without regard to a sovereign authority or the long-term consequences of one's actions). A child can also mature into *will-worship*, which is when a person who believes their ideology, religion or philosophy has absolute superiority and authority to rule over all life, rather than God or his son Jesus Christ who has sovereign authority above all life who has also been with us since the beginning of time – the creation (Genesis 1, KJV).

Therefore, because children are born with *free-will* into a sinful nature, children will mature into adults who will make their own choices, thus, being subjected to the environmental health impact of psychological, emotional harms of *free-will* and the sinful nature of other children and adults, which I further believe adversely affects a child's cognitive thinking and rationale causing distorted views within their life experiences. Consequently, as children mature, crime rates continue to rise because they will make ignorant harmful mistakes.

Yes, conceiving, giving birth, and raising a child can be a beautiful healthy experience for most women. It was a beautiful experience for me, too. But in contrast, there are *"44.7% of Black women, ages 15-50 years old," who are childless in the United States (https://www.statista.com/statistics/241538/percentage-of-childless-women-in-the-us-by-ethnic-group/)* due to miscarriages, elective abortions, sexual abstinence and infertility issues. Many other birth mothers have opted for adoption choosing not to embrace the physical and emotional responsibility of motherhood. But not every woman has had the choice of equality to choose what's best for her child. For instance – imagine being forced to become childless? Or, to give birth to five, ten or fifteen children, and watch your children stripped from your life and care, never having the opportunity to provide emotional support, love, protection, or ever hold her child again? Imagine that horror.

During the Atlantic slave trade (1619-1865), when African women were kidnapped from their homeland of Africa and forced into slavery here in the United States, some African women were hand-picked, examined by white physicians for white slave masters and forced to live in slave breeding farms to breed children with strange men, (African and White.) While enslaved, African women were forced to "birth more children into slavery" against their will while being sexually exploited, raped, taunted, and sexualized exposing them to physical and emotional turmoil.

Not excluding exposing them to sexually transmitted diseases and other illnesses such as: *"pneumonia, whooping cough, fever, cholera and helminthiasis." (Shared with permission: Center for Health Policy Studies, University of Texas School Public Health, University of Texas Health Science Center, Houston., www.ncbi.nlm.nih.gov), (https://www.ncbi.nlm.nih.gov/pmc/articles/PMC6167003/).*

"Thus, the value of these 'breeding women' at auction varied depending on whether enslavers viewed these women as the creator of potential lives and profit. In particular, slaveholding women saw value in these 'breeding women', and financially savvy white women purchased them with the intent to exploit their 'future increase."

Another historical example of how enslaved Black women were forced into the reproduction of children for their White slave masters:

"Many of these enslaved girls and boys were singled out as potentially productive producers and reproducers. Just as their enslavers had forced their parents to reproduce the labor force, they also forced the next generation to do so, too. Slaveholders forced mothers and fathers to witness their children experience the same violent and traumatic ordeal that they did — forced reproduction. Some enslaved men and women resisted forced reproduction through what has been termed 'reproductive resistance' – the use of natural contraceptives, long periods of nursing, abortions, and infanticide (4). However, those who did not choose or were unable to carry out this method of resistance witnessed their enslavers forcibly march their children down the same path they themselves were forced down. Life cycles and the reproduction of life was thus a huge part of enslaved peoples' day-to-day lives in the early- to mid-nineteenth century (5)." (Shared with permission: Written by Author, Aisha Djelid, and the source ("The master whished to reproduce": The (Forced) Reproduction of Enslaved Life in the Antebellum South, 1808-1865, published on the University of Reading Gender History Research Cluster blog, April 2021).

Consequently, *"in the South less than an estimated 50% of infants were stillborn or died within the first year of life." (Shared with permission: American Public Health Association, Diedra Cooper Owens, Department of History and Humanities in Medicine Program, University of Nebraska-Lincoln. Sharla M. Frett, History Department, Occidental College, Los Angeles, California., www.ncbi.nlm.nih.gov.)*

After the surviving infants were weaned from the birth mother, they were sold to strangers (e.g., abusive slave masters, criminals, and pedophiles) the birth mothers (whose names are a mystery) never to see their children again.

So, even if a woman is childless – or if she doesn't desire to conceive her own biological children, all women should be grateful for having the God given privilege and opportunity to become mothers whether the child is your biological child or not. Unable to conceive children, having your child kidnapped and sold, or abstaining from the experience of being a mother doesn't relieve women from motherhood. Why? Women were born to be mothers – to nurture the human race. That responsibility isn't going anywhere – ever, and it's not something to be ignored.

Unfortunately, for us human beings, one brief moment of deception within Eve's self-image of herself and her husband Adam was distorted by manufactured misguidance that changed the trajectory of the human race. God cursed women because of Adam and Eve's ungratefulness and greed. Eve was one of those rich Black women who had everything a woman could want but she was ungrateful and wanted more power than she could consciously bear.

The self-image of the woman has been distorted ever since Adam and Eve were banned from God's holy Garden of Eden. As a result, our ancestors suffered by the hands of American slavery which caused a great suffering in the Black lives of women, and now living beyond the memories of our ancestral history into the 21st century, how do Black women see the image of themselves?

We must acknowledge that we were born to be mothers – in this earth – in this African Diaspora – in America while maintaining the responsibility of reshaping our self-image. First reason – Black women have to accept the journey of motherhood and constantly repair the self-image of the Black woman to be seen as mothers in our own right and not as sex slaves forced to be mothers. Second reason– we have to work harder at maintaining everything: our beauty, family, education, employment, and spirituality. Why? Because Black women are the minority in America. We are women, and Black women. Third reason; the body is no longer pure and youthful because it ages. And, as the body ages, its appearance becomes distorted inwardly and outwardly– lumps and bumps, blemishes, sunburns, intellectual disfunctions such as dementia and Alzheimer's, hearing and vision loss is affected. Tiny waist lines expand into bus lines, our breasts lose their elasticity, instead they become shrinkage, and our menstrual cycles develop into menopause eventually restraining the woman's ovaries from ovulating no longer releasing human eggs to produce human life. Our bodies will function differently over time. Although natural, subsequently, as I mentioned previously, these issues do not relieve women from our duties of being mothers to the human race.

I know having pursued all that is perfect in an imperfect world doesn't make the world a perfect place because being a mother is a challenging laboring task. But, by obeying rational common sense, motherhood (maternal, foster or adopted) can be rewarding, too. A sense of gratification knowing she had the courage and inevitability to complete the task of a becoming a genuine mother.

With that said, pick up Eve's torch as a symbol of inspiration and strength, light it with a well-lit flame that never burns out, to give women all over the world, faith. Even though life on earth for human beings is still troublesome in the 21st century, in contrast, the book of Genesis, 1400, B.C., (Before Christ) explains how Eve stepped out into a cold [world of wandering] with her [moral] crown – her birthright to the purpose that she was chosen for – having no idea if her wandering in this new land would ever produce a viable path, nor was she prepared for the horrific challenges she faced as a mother having her oldest son Cain who became a fugitive who murdered her youngest son Abel; her sons and daughters to also become lovers, husbands and wives of each other; then Eve conceiving and birthing more daughters who also became mothers, etc., she persevered.

All women, because we are mothers, must embrace the correct path of refuge, a saving grace for our lives to thrive and to avoid further perpetual suffering that diminishes and destroys the quality of human life.

An African Violet symbolizes the strength and beauty in endurance. If cared for properly in the right climate, with good soil, water, and just enough sunlight, it has the vitality to live for many years on most continents throughout the world. In contrast, when a woman endures, she not only learns to survive, she thrives. Her strength is in how she was rooted and planted in her faith to endure a sincere, authentic commitment and devotion to her life's destiny.

~Felice Bois

Who Is She?

Mama, momma, mom, mother, I am a Black woman, all of them — Queen titles; an African American creole Modern Day Black Momma® within the African Diaspora. I have lived in this movement of cultural displacement here in America all of my life.

One morning, while giving birth in an Oakland, California hospital, my mother pushed and pushed until my tiny little body was encapsulated with new fresh air from this big old world. The doctor slapped me on my yellow rear-end to stimulate my first breath, I guess my eyes opened — then the doctor said "it's a girl."

My mother once told me she was happy she birthed a baby girl and named me "Felicia" because my birth name means "happy."

I was Born a bastard child of an adulterous affair, to a sixteen-year-old teenage mother, in the late-1960s, whose presence and love was sporadic throughout my childhood and to a young famous Oakland, California pimp, who taught me two things: when I was ten years old, he taught me how to spell my last name correctly, and as I matured into my adolescent years, he told me to dump abusive men.

My life experiences have been traumatizing and sweet. But, despite my psychological and emotional conflicts, my spiritual journey has been exceptionally interesting and rewarding. The Holy Trinity is my spiritual preference: God, His son Jesus Christ and the Holy Spirit. Furthermore, I believe in the Holy Bible: King James Version, which I truly believe was inspired by God. I also believe in living a purpose driven life, starting over on a clean slate and building up other people because I have been broken, I am fragile and an imperfect woman.

One hot sunny morning, I was anxiously glaring through our kitchen window while waiting to meet the man who prepared to introduce himself to me as my biological father. When he arrived, he drove up and parked his shiny dark blue 1979 Cadillac Eldorado in front of our long driveway which led to our upstairs apartment in Berkeley, California near Shattuck Avenue. As he got out of his car, I saw that he was a handsome, young, tall and slender light skinned Black man, with a big black afro, a thick mustache, sideburns and deep brown colored eyes. He wore a short dark leather jacket and dark flared men slacks. He stood with confidence, like he knew he was someone important. No big furs or bright colors, no fancy ladies waiting in his car, just him, he was alone.

As my father walked up the stairs, my mother opened the front door, he walked into our apartment, stood in the front door while briefly speaking with my mother – then they both looked at me, I looked at him, then he said "Yeah, you're my daughter." He walked closer to me, stooped down, looked me in my eyes and asked, "Can you read and write, Felicia?" I said "a little," (*I believe I was about nine or ten years old and could barely read and write*) he went on to ask me, "You know how to spell your last name?" I said "yes." Then he asked "How do you spell it?" I quickly went to my bedroom, grabbed some old schoolwork which had my first and last name written on it. Then, I handed my schoolwork to him, he looked at my handwriting (*which was sloppy and horrible and looked like a first-grader's handwriting*) and the spelling of my last name which was written and spelled so wrong I'm embarrassed to put it in this essay. Anyhow – then he said, "No, you're spelling your last name wrong."

"Go get me a pencil," he said. (*I could tell it bothered him that my handwriting and spelling was not good and my last name had been misspelled – pronounced correctly, but spelled wrong*). I rushed to the bedroom again and found a pencil and brought it to him. He then took the pencil and began to write the correct spelling of my last name while pronouncing each letter as he wrote them down on the paper. (*I won't spell it in this essay either because most people don't know how to pronounce my birth last name correctly.*) So, as he spelled my last name out loud to me, I copied him and wrote it down at the top of the page of my schoolwork and have spelled it correctly ever since that day.

About seven years later, when I was seventeen years old, my father visited my mother and me once again and sat at our kitchen table in our little rented house in Pittsburg, California, and said "Felicia, never let a man beat on you, he'll keep doing it."

It was weird listening to him speak to me as we both pierced our eyes at each other across our wooden kitchen table. Wow, I barely knew my father and he traveled all the way from the San Francisco Bay Area to give me dating advice – life advice. I thought it was cool and admirable considering I didn't know him well, and it had been over six years since I was first introduced to him. And, at that time, after growing up between my biological family and various fosters homes until age twelve, being the oldest sibling of three in a single parent low-income household, and a high school student on the verge of being a high school drop-out, I was just a modest, introverted young girl who knew nothing more than street life.

My mother called him to help me because I was dating a vicious, cold, brutal dude who was very abusive to me physically and verbally (my misfortune, and only bad date). I was trapped in a stereotypical domestic violence relationship as a pregnant unwed teenage girl with a man who did not respect or love me.

And, not too long after my father's visit, a tall Caucasian Contra Costa County Sheriff came to my aid after I fought off my abuser once again while seven months pregnant. The Sheriff sat at the same kitchen table as my father did with my mother and me and said "You can't keep allowing this guy to hit on you; he won't stop until you leave him." He spoke sincerely with compassion regarding my abusive circumstance. I believed him.

Of course, I knew my father and the Sheriff were giving me healthy advice, but I still didn't know how to leave and protect myself. But, five months later, after my near-death sentence during the premature labor of my first-born child, with my unhealed emergency cesarean section (C-section) and surgical staples still in place on my womb, several more blows to my head, arms, chest, and several fractured ribs, I knew my first born and I would be starting our new lives alone like white rice without the chicken gravy, it just wasn't going to be good. I left my abuser to stagger in his bitterness as I moved on to build a new life of my own by the age of 20. My body healed but that abusive violent relationship has forever scarred my spirit.

Time – so much time has passed – seconds, minutes and years later – my every thought has continued to unwind from my adolescent years. I have endured the trials and tribulations of growing and living in my own womanhood, being the eldest of my two siblings, a mother of two adult children and a wife. And, as I am writing this introduction, two of my dearest loved ones are doing hard time, 25-to-life in two of California's maximum state prisons. My daughter on the other hand, who is in her early twenties, a college student, a recreational pianist, roller-skater, singer-songwriter, is still learning how to adjust the reverb and power in her voice as her personality matures into womanhood.

In short, it took me years to understand the depth of the Modern Day Black Momma® beyond the appearance of my long skeleton torso, the sunrise color of my skin, the shape of my nose, my pointy ears, my high cheek bones, my almond shaped eyes, my lips, my curvy hips beneath my afflicted womb where I once carried my two children; the reflections and tones of my speech, the textures of my hair and the labor of my fingerprints, somehow, the Gospels of Jesus Christ, snatched my once lost soul on the breezy west coast of the globe, in Oakland, the Northern side of California in a cornerstone missionary Baptist church on 91st and International Boulevard.

Jesus Christ called me and saved me. He saved my soul. He pulled back the layers of my sickly, pulsing broken heart. I tried to create a new life of my own, but despite my genuine efforts – it was the living water (Jesus) that gave me a new life – he cleansed me, all the dark clouds and uncertain years of my future and despair suddenly became clear. It was April 7th, 1999, during morning church service. I was baptized with a five-month-old fetus in my womb – an unwed single mother-to-be. The spirit of God was with me in the water pulling back layers and rivers of my past sins. There were no fig leaves or clothes to cover the shame of my past lustful desires, my angry thoughts, the weight of unforgiveness I had towards others who intentionally caused me great pain and emotional grief. A great weight of sorrow each day that I lived was lifted. Jesus saw me – [He] knew me – my sins and years of my tears. He uncovered me. All my secrets were exposed and my loneliness was authentically bared. I was naked, but redeemed.

This was a sincere moment in a day of repentance for me. Prior to this day, I only understood life in terms of live, survive, lose and die. I grew up lost and confused in the middle. It was on this day, I told myself, that my existence on earth meant more to me than the suffering afflicted upon me or any pain I have ever inflicted on others. Which allowed me to escape the consequences of living in the strength of my own *free-will* (*living aimlessly, sinfully and within human limits*) within a world where I was forced to learn to live, survive, thrive and maintain for a future which was not promised to me.

Eventually, I learned to speak, crawl and walk again into my new life– I became a new person "*a new creature,*" (2 Corinthians 5:17, KJV). Then the eyes to *my* soul were opened. I knew there was nothing I could hide from God, at any time. And, I have never seen myself or any other woman the same, ever again.

Even as some of my imperfections continued to reveal themselves and challenge my personal character, I had constant correction through the Gospels of Jesus Christ. Since then, I have never been alone throughout any trials I have suffered but have learned to conquer through much prayer.

Respectfully, each time, I see a Black woman, I ask myself, well "Who Is She?" She is either a reflection of my past of being ignorantly and eternally lost, a glimpse of hope for a promising future she's been fighting for, or a woman whose external beauty is a reflection of the inner peace of her spirit. Perhaps, she is one of the millions of street walking prostitutes or a dancing stripper who freely bares her body and boldly sacrifices an intimate piece of her soul to strangers fascinated by a temporary fix of instant sexual gratification and adult entertainment.

Maybe she's the woman pushing her life's worth in a metal basket day in and day out because of chronic homelessness; sleeping in homeless camps, abandoned homes, public parks, alleys, dark corners, broken down cars, or sleeping under bridges at night which is unsafe for any woman. She could be trapped in the claws of her Suga daddy whose only true interest is to keep her mind and body captive for his own pleasure and to the detriment of her damaged self-esteem.

Whoever she is, she is a mirror of all Black women with stories untold; silent or stifled by the demands of life, unfiltered, raw and unfolding like mine. She could be a mother, grandmother, an aunt, daughter, sister, a cousin, close friend or any other Black woman, who unbeknownst to her, is revolutionizing the former African chattel slave into a subtle but brutally honest voice, shamelessly beautiful power and resilient strength who is a Modern Day Black Momma®.

My mother was born free, my grandmother, my great grandmother, and yes, I was born free, too, here in the United States of America. We are African American descendants of former chattel slaves who were enslaved (within the African Diaspora, outside of the African continent) in confederate states within the states of Texas, Louisiana, North Carolina, Alabama, Georgia, and the state of California. Further lineage descends from the continent of South America which includes the West Indies, part of the Caribbean countries of Trinidad and Tobago.

California was declared a free state on September 9, 1850, however, two years prior, California's dogma politics legally permitted chattel slavery and gold mining during the California Gold Rush, which eventually ended in 1855. For instance, "In 1848 when the gold rush hit, white southerners flocked to the state with hundreds of enslaved black people, forcing them to toil in gold mines, often hiring them out to cook, serve, or perform a variety of labor. Sometimes fortunes were amassed on the backs of this free labor." (Shared with permission. Author, Susan D. Anderson, "California, a 'Free State' Sanctioned Slavery," California Historical Society).

I'm thankful that the North won the Civil War and that Abraham Lincoln abolished slavery in America – thank God he signed the Emancipation Proclamation in July of 1863 (*I personally believe it was his true desire and his strategic plan prior to being elected as America's 16th president to end slavery in the United States*) – and that my family and I did not suffer direct spiritual deprivation, direct extreme physical poverty, or the direct harsh physical, psychological and emotional abuses by the hands of white supremacist slave masters who dominated and controlled the lives of African chattel slaves and their families daily. But, despite our physical freedom here in America, as free African Americans, and as direct beneficiaries of the Civil Rights movement, African Americans within the African Diaspora – we, including myself, have greatly suffered from the perpetuated extreme socioeconomic and environmental oppressive effects of slavery atrocities across the globe. Yes, still, right here in the state of California, in the hood. I have had to grow up and learn to survive and thrive in the aftermath of the authoritarian nature of slavery in the United States of America.

Understanding my ancestral history has helped me tremendously and gave me a deeper understanding for my purpose in life. When I was a young girl growing up, I have always had a strong desire to understand the omnipresence of the existence of pain and suffering, happiness and sadness, rich and poor. My desire for a deeper understanding allowed me to see the affects that each symptom that existed had on the condition of human life in the African American culture. And, how these symptoms within the human condition affected my life moments and environments around me growing up.

Moments like this is what I am living for– an implicit understanding of human life first, as a child of God, a Black woman and Black mother – that's what I like about myself. I have learned to understand myself through my desire to see my life through the lens of God, the dimensions of my ancestral history and through my DNA.

My life feeds and thrives on getting to the place of knowing me within my own universe at whatever levels of the hemisphere's life will take me – not separate from God but the just knowing of me.

Distractions attempt to deter me at times, but I am careful to discern the invisible arrows of my day-to-day life. And, by no means do I allow those invisible arrows to diminish my self-worth; instead, they have helped strengthen my faith in God. My faith in God is not an illusion or diluted by my short comings or my encounter with the evils within the world. My faith is difficult during trying moments, but it's constant.

And, despite my personal adversities and the global atrocities of Black women and the Black family, not excluding the generational blows we still suffer and tolerate, which perpetuated the war on mental health, the war on drugs, the war on guns and the war on sex trafficking – we, Black women, continue to endure in *any* way, even with our own personal demons. Still, we are learning to persistently rise above the perpetuity of our physical and emotional tyrannies because the demands of life command that we do.

World history has taught us that Black women and the Black family were worthless unless someone owned us, or controlled our assets, our future, when in fact we are truly intelligent, beautiful Black Queens, and Princesses who were meant to be free to find our own paths. We are relevant and priceless women who were already crowned with purpose in our birthright.

When God created us in our mother's wombs, He was there with us as Black women when He created women to be wives, mothers, leaders, teachers, and entrepreneurs. He was there when some Black women chose the alternative road instead: to become thieves, liars, whores, cheaters, murderers, abusers, and bullies! And, He is still with Black women regardless of our economic status.

I would like to encourage you to examine your spirit. Know who you are, go learn who are and don't forget where you come from and to control the avenues life presents to you. Every woman must have a sense of self-awareness (*understand your ancestral history, spirituality, personality and what defines your individuality*) to understand your past, the present, and your future, to help shred layers of vanity (*material things*), withered dreams (dreams that never come into realization), illusionary hopes (*irrational desires of things that will never happen because it doesn't make sense. Not logical*) and unwarranted high expectations (*expecting to complete something that is impossible to achieve*) of yourself or attempts to over-achieve.

Plant good healthy seed in your mind and heart to grow new branches of green leaves, the green leaves represent your new life and healthy spirit within yourself.

As you plant a new healthy spirit within yourself, get your "flowers" while making conscious progress. Invest in regular intentional self–care, such as having access to indoor or outdoor flowers. Don't wait for flowers to be given to you. Grow or buy your own bouquet of fresh beautiful flowers to boost your self-esteem and mood, as often as you can - doing so, adds value to your self-worth.

For instance, I recently read an online article*: Positive Mental Health Benefits of Flowers, According to Science -* says*:* "The 'flower power' test found some interesting results for how it helped boost people's moods: 90% said they found focusing on something creative helped to reduce their stress levels.

84% said flowers had an overall calming effect on their mood.

53% said they felt relaxed or at ease when arranging flowers.

There's a breadth of scientific evidence supporting the idea that connection with nature has important therapeutic benefits for human mental health." (Shared with permission. For more information go to: www.psychreg.org.)

Flowers are symbolically used to celebrate the life or loss of life of someone, birthdays, weddings, special events, or to enhance room decor. So, as long as you live, earn your flowers and celebrate your life, anytime, any day, not just holidays or birthdays. Oh, there's one catch to buying a fresh bouquet of flowers, depending on the brand - they die within one to two weeks after you bring them home.

Seasonal or perennial flowers have short lifespans such as roses and carnations. A renewed season allows them to grow back allowing for an extended lifespan. But, as long as they have water and the light needed for energy, they will grow, blossom and live, but they still die. The human life span is almost identical except humans live much longer, however in death, the physical body and soul does not reincarnate.

Here's another quick example: You are the flower. For as long as you water yourself in the sunlight, bringing in new energy and new strength, you will grow, blossom, live and thrive, but at some point, you will also feel extremely fatigued or as though the body is dying. That's because the symptoms of life attack the living-water within the body daily. In essence, the living-water is Jesus Christ (John 4:14, KJV) and as long as you have the living-water, you have life. Re-water and rehydrate yourself. Take baby steps or jump right on in and consider reinventing yourself with a new perspective on life.

Read books. Read books about finance and real estate to build wealth, and books about life science to understand the physiology of the human body, sociology to understand the condition of human society and books about Black history to understand your race, lineage and ancestral history, or storytelling illustrated through colorful animation to further engage and reward your interest in reading.

Book reading promotes "deep reading" according to a scientific study published in the National Library of Medicine and is preferred compared to reading magazines, newspapers and periodicals. "The findings suggest that the benefits of reading books include a longer life in which to read them," in addition "reduces the risk of mortality."

An example of "deep reading," in my opinion, would be to find a quiet place to read books concerning meaningful topics that truly engage your whole spirit to learn, enjoy and maximize what is being read.

By the way, deep reading is something I practice often to destress while escaping everyday people, social media and television; in addition to that, deep reading allows me to create a new atmosphere, a more fulfilling and engaging experience away from day-to-day life.

Furthermore, *"cognitive engagement may explain why vocabulary, reasoning, concentration, and critical thinking skills are improved by exposure to books.* More equally important, *"books can promote empathy, social perception, and emotional intelligence, which are greater processes for greater survival."* (Shared with permission. Authors: 1Yale University School of Public Health, Laboratory of Epidemiology and Public Health, 60 College Street, New Haven, CT 06510. Masters in Chronic Disease Epidemiology, Copyright, July 18, 2016, https://www.ncbi.nlm.nih.gov/pmc/articles/PMC5105607/).

In the meantime, consider learning how to pray (everybody aint praying for you — learn to pray for yourself), eat healthy tasty foods, wear new colors, meet new good people in a safe manner, support a meaningful cause, start a new career or answer a calling that ignites passion and purpose for your life, join a fitness club, learn a new hobby such as cooking (*new cuisines*), sewing, music, dancing, drawing, writing, swimming or gardening. Ride bikes, visit art and history museums, learn to crochet, create handcrafted jewelry or see a stage play. Attend motivational seminars or webinars that inspires the transformation of people who desire to improve upon their lives.

Control your thoughts. If you need help or know another woman who needs help, talk to a trusted friend, a professional licensed psychologist or mental health therapist; consider speaking to a respected pastor or first lady of a bible teaching church. Learn to work through

adversities that trigger negative thoughts in your mind (*e.g., find a safe private space to work through difficult life moments and gather your emotions*) and learn to build yourself up from those negative thoughts and heartaches of life that have attacked your self-esteem and abandoned you in that pain.

Need to cry? Cry. Tears can release the aggravations of life that have caused so much pain and suffering. Crying is an excellent coping strategy which is a natural attribution to your emotional and physical wellbeing.

An article published by Harvard Health Blog, "Is Crying Good for You?" written by Leo Newhouse, LICSW, contributor, who is a Senior Social Worker in Neurology at Beth Israel Deaconess Medical Center, wrote: "Today's psychological thought largely concurs, emphasizing the role of crying as a mechanism that allows us to release stress and emotional pain". He further explains that "Crying is an important safety valve, largely because keeping difficult feelings inside – what psychologist call repressive coping – can be bad for your health". (Shared with permission, Harvard Health Publishing. For more information go to www.health.harvard.edu.)

Absolutely, I agree with Mr. Leo Newhouse. Personally, I cry whenever necessary to cope with my emotional and physical pain. I can't imagine life without tears – they internally cleanse the anatomy of the human *soul* – the mind, heart, emotions and the human will.

Re-watering yourself like a flower reinvigorates your life. Fresh water with flowers breathes new life in any atmosphere. More importantly, when you shine, people around you will shine, too.

Oh, one more thing: Authors, physicians, counselors, preachers, motivational speakers, celebrities, relatives, best friends, spouses, co-workers, next-door neighbors, the package delivery person and please – don't ask the garbage man – neither of these people can help solve your day-to-day life challenges. Don't expect these people to pick up a magic wand and go "ding" "problem solved" no – that is an unnatural process of life.

True, some problems are easier to solve and others lengthier and more challenging. Without a doubt, it is the efforts of the pursuer – you – the woman (*the person seeking help for the inspiration, motivation and transformation*) must educate herself and connect with people or resources, online or locally, as I mentioned previously, to help understand [how] to solve your problems, establish healthy wisdom in your mind and heart to achieve a fulfilling future.

Modern Day Black Momma®

Who Is She?

Who is the Modern Day Black Momma®?

originally free

torn from Africa

groomed into an American slave

somebody saw

through her dark skin

their American dream

a cultural genocide

stripped her authenticity

her family, broken, by greed

self-identity,

 family values and traditions

she struggled to hold

freedom for her family

freedom they got

for those who wanted it

scattered abroad

livin' Afro-Euro

holdin' on to the

underground railroad

negro mother's dream

the Modern Day Black Momma®

who is she, today?

she's the thriving successful business woman

the career mother struggling with corporate racism

she's momma and daddy sometimes rolled in one

she's

the songstress longing for a hit solo

tryin' to sing away her blues

but procrastination redirects her dreams

she's the divorcee looking for romance—

her mental baggage is too heavy

to embrace new relationships

momma is the beauty shop gossip queen

braiding, weaving, pressing and perming hair

chatting with clients

she hopes will continue to bring in the revenues

she's the waitress in the restaurant

the cashier at the local grocers

the banker who cashes your neighbor's paycheck

rejected by a society

who says:

she ain't pretty enough

ain't light enough

ain't dark enough

too fat, too thin

hair ain't straight or kinky enough

unpolished English

you know – the fictitious beauty queen

we ain't gone neva see

she's

the mother who shuffles between work and welfare -

struggling

to find herself in a world that does not understand

she's the mother

living in low-income housing—

she ain't got enough money

to pay rent on her own

workin'

getting' letters in the mail

sayin'

"yo' bills are still past due"

she's the mother

who frequents juvenile courts

to rescue her rebellious son

she's

the Modern Day Black Momma® who arrives to
the church house

seeking answers to her problems

and consolation from the Word of God

sanity, cancer, AIDS

she's still fightin'

pushin for her life

she is

the personification of the ghetto queen

a leader in her community

with painted acrylic nails, hair styles,
fashions and figures that become a
phenomenon

she's the one with the fancy church
hat—

with a décor of diamonds and gold

on hands that labored for years

she's

the bus driver,

the construction worker even the
postman

the police officer and the judge

who must jail their own

she is the MBA entrepreneur

with an empire of ideas

the single parent re-entry student starting
over—

parenting demanded her attention in her
teen years

she's the teacher who empowers the
mind,

the actress fighting for her role
the doctor, the lawyer

who graduated with honors and
credentials to carry her to the top

the first lady

whose skin tone they ain't neva seen as
the prime-time speaker

stretched center stage

of America

she's

the minister trying to save your soul,

the activist pounding on your door

saying "vote for your rights."

she is

the dancer who will never grace

the stage of an audience—

she lost her dance along the way

she's the prostitute

trying to escape an environment she's
addicted to

the drug addict - the thief

who got lost trying to find her way

she's

the momma whose been abused as a
small child,

damaged

and prone to domestic violence
relationships

she's the one with the mental problem

now a government responsibility—

the one holding it all together fighting for
both of your lives

she's the one reaching out

pulling you back and begging you

to stop and listen

she's

the first person the neighbors, relatives,
school officials, and police call

when our sons fall into trouble

I wondered if you knew

the Modern Day Black Momma®

Written by Felice Bois, ©2006

An Unbiased Human Experience

My dog died. I'm heart broken. Her name was Peaches. She was a beautiful Black female mixed short haired Chihuahua who lived on this earth for nine years. Sunset, August 1, 2023. I first held Peaches when she was eight weeks old. She was my family, my emotional support dog. I loved her and miss her.

During the month of December, fall season of 2014, two or three weeks before Christmas, an African American woman who lived a couple houses down was standing outside in her front yard, approached me as I was beginning my morning walk. She was holding a tiny black shivering puppy *(it was cold outside)* by its scruff in the palm of her hand, and asked "do you want a puppy?" I looked at the puppy, the puppy looked at me – the puppy's eyes and spirit were so engaging they caused a desire in me to want to hold it – so I rubbed the puppy's short black fur. It was friendly and cute! Before the woman handed the puppy to me, she said "wait – her name is Peaches, she's eight weeks old and a girl."

The woman explained that she wanted to give Peaches to someone that would give her a good home, and she further explained, that if Peaches wasn't a good fit in my home, I could return the puppy back to her. I eagerly agreed to adopt Peaches and to give her a good home. The woman trusted me – she didn't smile much – but she appeared to be a person of dignity and benevolence – someone who embodied respect and compassion for animals and human life – she was kind. She gently handed Peaches to me, and said "take care of her," I said, "I will take good care of her, thank you" as we parted paths. As I held Peaches close to me to keep her warm, I kissed her ear as I went back into my house to surprise my daughter CoraMay who was surprised and extremely happy to meet the new addition to our family. We liked the name Peaches, so we didn't change her name. Both my daughter and I had suffered unwarranted trauma years prior and were seeking refuge in peace and comfort and agreed that having a new puppy would enrich our lives. We didn't look back and had no regrets. Peaches was now our family.

We potty trained her pretty fast with the exception she'd pee and poop on my bed a couple times, until one day Peaches realized, she could either earn a "treat" or "no treat."

Her potty place was in our second-floor bathroom between our bedrooms which we kept newspaper on the floor. She was always happy after she peed or pooped - caught on fast and learned to whine and make eye contact with one of us, scratch the bathroom door or downstairs back door when ready to go outside to do the "number one" or the "number two."

We fed her healthy dog food and fresh water daily, socialized her with my nearby neighborhood dogs and felines. Didn't like big dogs too much because they towered over her little body and were intimidating, I guess. Maybe because she was so short.

Eventually, by age two, Peaches met Runakco, my daughters' new dog, a white mixed short haired Chihuahua, about the same age as Peaches – I think – eventually, they bred a litter of seven puppies. Two boy puppies died in birth, five puppies survived – two boys, three girls. Peaches loved her babies. But, after two to three months of weaning her litter of pups, I had to sell them.

They were precious and beautiful pups but five more dogs in the house were too many. We successfully found homes for two puppies and were left with three as seen in the picture, and eventually found the last three puppies' good homes.

Peaches was grateful to have a home, to be loved and welcomed. She enjoyed playing indoor fetch ball and being rewarded with treats, a smile or hug for doing something positive. She also learned how to pick up her leash on command and bring it to me to go outside for a walk.

Sometimes, a kiss on her ear or cheek is all she needed, a quick belly rub or a good bath or shower. Never too much affection, just enough to show that her life mattered.

She was always happy to see me walk through the front door after being gone for a few minutes to a couple hours; and she'd always tuck herself away under her blanket or sniff my feet as I put my clothes and shoes on because she could sense I was leaving for an extended period of time.

Peaches was an excellent watch dog. I felt safe with her in my home. She protected my home with a snappy sharp bark if someone rang the doorbell or lurked near our windows. She sensed all things around her in the most distracting and quietest moments. Foods like ground beef, chicken, liver and mixed veggies, especially raw yams, cucumber and watermelon were some of her favorite foods.

She gave me peace and space during lonely and nerve wrecking days when I needed it. Most days, she'd mind her own business. Her silence in some instances and presence added a higher degree of quality to my life. If I was having a bad moment at home, all she had to do is look at me. She was a caring still spirit who expressed concern about my life and my mood. Never judgmental. She would sit in her bed and stare at me, walk towards me or stand afar from me – give me a dog stare until I responded verbally or give her a stare back, which was a good distraction on my bad days.

There's nothing better than to have an emotional support animal whose personality and physical presence adds cushion that strengthened the mental and emotional stamina for my traumatized brain and heart. She taught me to appreciate life. I didn't realize what she was teaching me until the night we dug her three-deep grave.

After nine years of a happy home, like a lightning bolt, I watched her health rapidly decline, overnight and fade away – she was gone just that fast. Although, I wasn't sure, I sensed she was dying. She was sick, weak and wobbly when she walked short distances, refused all food and drank only water for a week and a half. The veterinarian believed Peaches suffered a heat stroke, as a result, damaged her organs. Medicine wasn't going to help. She was nine years old, and the heat affected her body differently than it did years prior.

On this particular day, August 1, 2023, most of the day she could barely stand on her own, she didn't want to stand on her own. I took her outside early during the morning sunrise. She walked a little but she didn't like it. I had to carry her back into the house. She sipped a little water like water wasn't water – like it was a foreign food. Laid her in her doggie bed to rest. I checked on her periodically.

Most of the day, she laid still in a deep trance – alive, but she wouldn't move much. She didn't respond much to my voice either unless I touched her or picked her up to hug her – several times to be exact - I even cradled her tightly in my arms and allowed her to see me hug her in the mirror. I intentionally wanted her to have memories of affection. It was important for me to let Peaches die peacefully and knowing she was loved. I refused to let her die on her doggie bed, under my bed, in a corner, a shelter or veterinarian office. She deserved to rest in peace respectfully knowing that her life and legacy meant something to me.

The sun was still shining over my bed and I remember removing Peaches from her doggie bed – hugged her and let her see herself in the mirror one more time – then I kissed her on her ear. I believe she felt loved and cared for but her spirit was sad. I put Peaches onto the left side, foot end of my bed, near the window, so she could enjoy the cool air and the dusk of the sunshine.

Kissed her cheek, rubbed her fur and her belly and she laid there still, quiet and rested. But still awake and alive. It was getting late and I was emotionally exhausted, so I doubled checked my front door, made sure it was locked, then laid down on the front end of my bed on my pillow but close enough to check on Peaches. We slept in early around 6:30 PM for several hours. When I woke, around 9:50 P.M., I looked over my shoulder to peek at Peaches, her soul had gone out of her – she was lifeless.

Riga mortis had begun to settle In her stiffening body. Right next to me, my Peachy died in peace. She was not alone. Once I realized she had passed, I got up off my bed, I stood there in awe – in silence, towering over her lifeless little body to confirm her death with the touch of my right hand – there was no life and no heartbeat. As I stood there, grabbed my cell phone, then I took a couple of pictures of her lifeless body and created a 21 second video to memorialize my final memories of her. I just needed those few moments alone with her before I contacted anyone – about five minutes or so. Shortly, thereafter, I was still in disbelief, but I knew it was real so I called my daughter to notify her of Peaches' death.

When my daughter arrived, she rushed over and grieved the death of Peaches loudly. She loved Peaches. Peaches loved her, more. I had not mourned Peaches' death in tears yet because I was still in shock and trying to figure out what to do with her body. She was dead on my bed. So, I gathered my thoughts and called the non-emergency police, and told them I didn't know what to do with my dogs' dead body. The operator encouraged me to give Peaches a "proper burial" – I did what she said to do.

I had not prepared or literally buried a beloved animal before, so we contacted a close friend of the family who offered to allow us to bury Peaches on his land, an exclusive very large private back yard, rarely used. We accepted his offer. I gathered my thoughts and calmed my daughter's spirits. CoraMay did not understand the process of death yet, she was afraid to touch Peaches' lifeless body; so, I explained to my daughter, although her spirit and soul are gone out of her body, it was safe to touch her, and she had only been dead maybe a couple hours. As she gleamed and stood over Peaches' lifeless body, my daughter grieved loudly and stroked her black fur one last time.

Preparing for Peaches' burial. As my daughter's friend waited for us outside, calmly, I lightly wrapped Peaches in her favorite pink doggie paw blanket (the blanket she died on). I grabbed my purse, phone and house keys. My daughter locked my house door. As I carried Peaches outside and approached the car, I notice that the car trunk was wide open. My daughter's friend instructed me to put Peaches in the car trunk because he didn't want a dead dog in his nice car. No complaints here, I was happy to have the help. Slowly and carefully, I laid Peaches in the dark car trunk, wrapped in her pink blanket with a large shovel, gas can, some car tools, and flashlights. I made sure her body was flat and covered securely with her blanket. She was beautiful and still. After I secured her body, I closed the car trunk, got into the car, strapped my seat belt on and we all drove quietly to a private burial spot.

After we arrived, it was very dark. Our only source of light were several bright flash lights and the headlights from the car. As my daughter's friend dug the deep grave, I removed Peaches' dead weight body from the car trunk and laid her on the dirt ground, still inside her pink doggie blanket, uncovered to allow our other two dogs to grieve the death of her. They sniffed Peaches pretty good, all over her. Especially her face and the tail end. The dogs continued to circle her body until they accepted her death as they were saddened and wondered away from her body, they knew she was dead.

The fresh burial was ready. We looked over Peaches' body one more time, told her we loved her and how precious she was to us. Then I wrapped her body loosely and tight enough to secure her body in her doggie blanket one more time. She was getting heavy. I was nervous and scared to bury Peaches. In my mind, I was thinking…. "What if she wasn't really dead?" "What if my dog is still breathing?" I quickly snapped out of my disbelief and realized it wasn't a good time to have an anxiety attack so I quickly pulled my emotions together to focus on the burial.

She was dead. As I held Peaches in the palm of my hands, I walked closer to her burial site, and gently placed her in the deep three-foot hole, still in her pink doggie blanket. My daughter and the two other dogs stood afar and watched. I said a quick little prayer over Peaches, then my heart sank. I was afraid to cover her with the burial dirt and leave her there. But we covered her little body until we couldn't see her anymore. I tightly packed the dirt to make sure she was buried properly and that her body was secure in the ground. I still couldn't believe I was burring Peaches.

The burial dirt was finally packed pretty tight. My daughter held a large square beaming flash light over Peaches' grave as her friend helped me cover it with small and large stone rocks. The rocks were arranged neatly over her grave site. We were finished - said our last goodbyes, grabbed our flash lights, the shovel and our two other dogs and got into the car.

The red break lights from the car lit up Peaches' grave site as we began to drive away. And, the car head lights guided us out of the large private yard into a very large front yard full of large green trees.

We left Peaches in the ground, in the dark. Alone. She went back to the dirt she came from and to our God who created her. All we have left are memories, pictures and videos of our lives with her. We have her legacy.

The following day my daughter went back to Peaches' grave site and signed the stone rocks for us and made the grave site look a little neater. Because during her burial, we weren't focused on the aesthetics of her grave site too much but our grieving and giving her a decent burial with respect and dignity was our priority.

Nine years of my life were filled with irreplaceable memories of a dog that enriched my wellbeing. I can't take Peaches on her morning walks anymore, I will never hear her bark when the doorbell rings, or when the mailman or the delivery guy arrives. I will never hear her whine for a treat or demand that I get out of my bed early in the morning, she will never pick–up her leash again. But knowing she was a pleasure to have around and that my house was her house, I have no regrets about including her in our lives – she was my piece of freedom in America. And, her death immediately reminded me to appreciate life experiences that allowed me to have an unbiased human experience.

Peaches and I had a great human-animal bond; she filled a void in my life when my expectations of humans were incapable of healing my wounds and past traumas. And, me, never fully expecting the presence of an animal could help patch up my emotional and psychiatric woes would have a lasting impact. She didn't care if I was fat or skinny, if my hair was straight, nappy, short or long. She did not care about the color of my hair, or if my skin was White, Black, freckled or Brown, if I was short, tall or thin. I didn't have to be popular, rich or have a high-end job in a skyscraper commercial building with a view overlooking the San Francisco Golden Gate Bridge.

She never judged me but allowed me to be human – myself, every day. I allowed Peaches to be herself – a dog, every day because she was my road dog. A road dog is not there to deceive you, cause harm to you, delay or interfere with your destination. They dive in the trenches – with you – and pump more life in the life you already have. They never judge you because they have learned to understand the struggle of your highs and lows. Your road dog may not be an animal – it may be a person you've grown to love and respect and vice versa. If you don't have a road dog, it's okay to ride alone. But, if you do have one, make sure they always have your back. When you look left, your road dog should be looking right. You look up, they should be looking down. You fall backwards – then your road dog should be standing right behind you – to catch you. Fall forward, then your road dog should be looking you in the eyes while saying – "I got you".

Even Jesus didn't walk alone. He had His Father God in heaven and His disciples while on earth. Yes, He died on the cross alone because that was God's plan for His life was to redeem, restore dignity and respect within the human race – to save our souls – because we have all been messy sinners at some point in our lives. You have to follow Gods plan for *your* life. And, if you don't know God, you better hurry and meet Him – your life's journey has already begun – its final destination is determined by the choices you make for your future now. If you haven't met Him – you are walking in complete darkness – you are lost! Wrong road – detour! You are on the A-list of lost people. Even during the best moments of your life – you are on the wrong road – with the wrong map – and wrong directions. Stop walking around earth like you don't need help from people. Got it? Good.

I know someone reading this might say, "Well, Felice – I don't have a road dog, I don't need one, or many friends at all and I really don't care what people think of me – I don't care who's judging me." Then, I would say: "that's your rightful prerogative." You might be in a place of neutrality learning to adjust to an adversity that's impacting your personal or professional progress, or maybe you've created a new or updated vision board, written a new business plan, enrolled in college as a new or reentry student preparing for a dynamic career, which is plausible – it sounds great. And, I don't want to forget women who are fresh out of federal and state prisons (throughout the world) – your chains, handcuffs and crimes are of the past. New fresh concrete ground – new beginnings are good and being alone for a while is even better – for a little while – as needed. But, at some point in your life journey you will need help from other people. They will either support you or harm you – they see you and meet you where you are emotionally, spiritually and intellectually. Those people will be your road dogs, beginning within a few seconds, to a few minutes, months and even years. A handshake, a smile, a kiss, a hug, money, directions or whatever they have to offer, whomever these people will become in your life, whether short term or for the long haul, they will play a significant role in helping to bring balance in your life and to help carry out your decisions that will forever impact your life journey.

Some of these road dogs will be good people, bad people, and pretense (confused) people. Find the good people fast because you can only trust the bad people for a little while and the pretense people will disappear without notice. My suggestion is simply this – stop giving time to people, places or things that don't help make you whole or better and they do nothing to improve the longevity of your livelihood, because every good and bad thing that enters your life will leave a lifelong impression before it exits.

Peaches and I had a great human-animal bond. She was our family, beautiful spirit and dedicated road dog. We will forever miss her hugs and your bath-tub dances. *(Peaches loved taking baths. After she bathed, she would get out the tub and doggie dance).*

According to a recent scientific research article published by the National Library of Medicine: "The Role of Human–Animal Bonds for People Experiencing Crisis Situations" explains "Human-animal bonds have been associated with improvements in human health."

Furthermore, *"Human-animal bonds provide social support to human beings, reducing anxiety, depression, and stress." (Shared with permission. Authored by: Conceptualization, K.O. and G.M.; methodology, K.O., J.R. and G.M.; formal analysis, K.O., J.R. and G.M.; data curation, K.O. and G.M.; writing—original draft preparation, K.O.; writing—review and editing, J.R., S.L., B.H. and G.M.; supervision, S.L., B.H. and G.M. 1. Karl Oosthuizen, Sydney School of Life and Environmental Science, Faculty of Science, The University of Sydney, Camperdown, NSW 2006, Australia, 2. Bianca Haase, Sydney School of Veterinary Science, Faculty of Science, The University of Sydney, Camperdown, NSW 2006, Australia, 3. Jioji Ravulo, Sydney School of Education and Social Work, Faculty of Arts and Social Sciences, The University of Sydney, Camperdown, NSW 2006, Australia, 4. Sabrina Lomax, Royal Society for the Prevention of Cruelty to Animals New South Wales, 201 Rookwood Rd, Yagoona, NSW 2199, Australia, Gemma Ma., Copyright, March 1, 2023., https://www.mdpi.com/2076-2615/13/5/941).*

R.I.P. Peaches. Thank you for being light for those who never knew you. ~Granny.

Conquer the Bitter Black Curse: The Wandering Black Woman's Self-Image

It's not too cold outside this morning. A few white clouds, no sign of rain, but today's weather is cooling. I feel relaxed. Early mornings are moments when I'm able to have deep self-reflection which allows me to reflect on my past most often and my future. Prayer has always been the best method of bringing forward my day and a cup of hot ground chicory. It has a chocolaty and a slight hint of mint flavor that stimulates my endorphins because of its calming affects, it's more satisfying than a cup of coffee. The smell of hot chicory, the flavor and hot steam are a perfect combination with this morning's weather and the matters of my heart. So, let's get into this next topic which I believe will be quite stimulating and rewarding for the most part for Black women who wish to refine their own lives because maybe she's been that Wandering Black Woman who forgot where she came from or she never knew where she was going.

This self-love essay has allowed me to weave together fabrics of the life of my past, who I am now and my future. It is my warmest wish that this self-love essay will encourage other Black women to begin weaving in the fabrics of everything that defines her life in the past, her life now, and her future to breathe life into an honest meaningful narrative of herself.

Some of the sharpest, richest, most beautiful Black women – all women on earth can trace her ancestral history back to slavery, the American and international ghettos. So, to be clear, this section of my self-love essay is not specifically about Black women who have been deprived spiritually, financially or intellectually, but about the past, present condition and trajectory of the Black woman's self-image.

So, what is the Bitter Black Curse: The Wandering Black Woman's Self-Image?

The Bitter Black Curse is a dark spirit that forms a crack in the human mind, the physical body, and the human spirit with the intentions to destroy. It can affect any human being – a man, woman or child, and animals in certain conditions. But, for the purposes of this self-love essay, I'm speaking specifically about Black women; however, any woman in the world could probably relate to a similar adversity.

Furthermore, the livelihoods of Black women were rooted and formed by the perpetuated effects of African ancestral atrocities, subliminal politics and racism in the African Diaspora. These atrocities have permeated from generation to generation through different groups of people in our communities with different beliefs, personalities, and different standards of living. As a result, the subliminal permeation of those African ancestral atrocities helped to shape the permanently fractured image of the Black woman. She's always at the recovery stage – someone is always coming to rescue the Black woman who is lost – wealthy, middle class or poor.

I'm going to share a few descriptive snapshots of my childhood, adolescence and young adulthood from the past to demonstrate the self-image of a Wandering Black Woman here in America.

Between 1968 and 1981, while residing in Alameda and Los Angeles County, periodically, I would live with my grandmother who was spiritually grounded, my mother, aunts, and a host of foster parents until the age of twelve.

As an elementary school student and foster child in the Oakland Unified School District, I've attended many schools because of home instability. The schools I attended back then, had decent physical dwellings, clean hallways, classrooms and bathrooms; the campuses were generally clean. Teachers had access to basic school materials to teach any young child who was ready and stable enough to learn.

School Bullies: During school recess, after lunch, I remember most kids would play kick ball, jump rope, hopscotch, twirl on the metal bars; or the boys would do front and back flips on the concrete. And, a great game of Jax was always fun, it was similar to rolling dice, except, the game of Jax included a small red ball with six or eight round, star shaped spiky objects made of plastic or metal. To win the game, the player had to roll the Jax on the ground until they spread out, then bounce the red ball in the air, while the ball was in the air, the player would have to grab as many Jax as possible and catch the red ball before it hits the ground. The kid who would get all their Jax off the ground before the other kid, would win the game.

Contrary to our high-energy recesses during class breaks, beginning with grades third to eighth grades, most Black kids in Oakland, California, had to fight other kids often to survive most days at school or get beaten-up or bullied by other kids. I have met some really mean messed up kids; and I've seen good Black kids get chased home by mobs of ghetto Black kids because the good kids were dressed well, smarter and well mannered.

The Black kids who were bullies were probably victims of physical and emotional abuse, too. I guess, their emotional pain or neglect fueled their lashing out at others— who knows, but in retrospect, it's what I believe and witnessed. As I advanced from elementary school to junior high school, and high school I saw the same problem repeating itself with more Black kids beating each other or causing emotional harm in the schools I attended.

The number of African American children with reports of abuse or neglect in the state of California, 2020, were 98.8 per 1000 children. (California Child Welfare Indicators Project, CCWIP Reports. University of California at Berkeley & California Dept. of Social Services [Oct. 2021], www.kidsdata.org, a program of Population Reference Bureau).

As a junior high school student, in seventh and eighth grades, at Central Junior High School, in Pittsburg, California, I had to fight more kids to survive – snatched my purse back from one chick who took it from me in the girl's locker room. Then, I had one fist fight in wood shop because a boy called me a dirty name; and another fist fight, after school in a dried-up, waterless canal adjacent to the school near the school walking trail, to protect my sibling. After a long exhausting fist fight in the canal, my opponent and I walked home together with the other school kids to our apartment complex, Woods Manor. I had two small knots on my forehead and my opponent – I left him with a large knot on his forehead. Some months later, I had another fist fight with another guy, and another one after that with a Mexican chick who was trying to scratch my eyes out, literally. I was tired of fighting to survive in the ghettos – everybody was mad each other. And, while living in Woods Manor, which was a low-income housing apartment complex with Blacks and Mexicans, we had to wake up to a boat load of roaches on the kitchen floor every day. Turn the kitchen lights off at night after cooking and cleaning– turn them back on after an hour, bang! Roaches scattered everywhere.

Bank Robbery: Then I had to watch a middle-aged Black man, who robbed the Wells Fargo bank down the street on E. Leland Rd. and Railroad Avenue – I watched him get shot and murdered after his failed bank robbery. He robbed the bank and a high-speed chase ensued. I could hear the police sirens as I rushed to the kitchen window. The bank robber, in a tan Buick, quickly parked his car in front of our apartment complex, jumped out, ran forward for a moment across the green grass with the money bag in his hands, when he then looked back– an Asian police officer shot him nine times in front of all the kids outside in broad daylight; I watched the devastation unfold. We were stunned. The bank robber died – he was unarmed.

Taking a step back for a moment. As an elementary student in the Oakland Unified School District, I really didn't learn much until I reached the sixth grade at Golden Gate Elementary. I had an African American teacher named Ms. Brown who always encouraged her students to read; she formed reading groups for her students during class time and encouraged us to read aloud to each other – we all struggled to read. In fact, in third grade I could barely read and write or form a sentence; my handwriting looked like that of a kindergartener's. For instance, I remember when my mother was home temporarily to care for my sibling and I, it was during my third-grade promotion to fourth grade. While standing in the school hallway, in front of my class door, my mother was having a discussion with my teacher about my academic performance. After the teacher showed her a paper with my handwriting, which had sloppy unformed penmanship, misspelled words and incomplete sentences, in that moment, my mother learned that I could barely read and write. So, she then instructed the teacher to keep me in the third grade which is why I was always a grade behind in school from then on. And, before I was eighteen years old, I was a high-school drop-out and a single parent with one child. I had been physically abused a lot growing up – punched, beat in my back and left with purple and green bruises on some occasions. But, thank God for my grandmother, Lannie and blessing oil. *"In California only 33.8 percent of African American students in grades 3, 4, 5, 6, 7, 8 and 11th grades met or exceeded the grade level standard in English Language Arts (ELA), which means 66.2 percent have not met or are exceeding in reading and writing. This result can negatively impact preparation for college or work readiness in the real world."* (California Dept. of Education, Test Results for California's Assessment, [February 2022], www.kidsdata.org, a program of Population Reference Bureau).

Random Moments While in Foster Homes:

Kids Playing with Guns

While in foster care, somewhere in Alameda or Los Angeles County, I was five or six years old, my African American childhood neighbor shot me in my right foot with a long barrel BB gun. He was twelve years old. We were all (kids) outside playing in the backyard, and he (the twelve-year-old) had this long Black rifle looking gun. He was bragging about the BB gun to the younger kids and myself

and explained to us that BB guns don't hurt and then asked me if I wanted to see what it felt like by shooting my foot. I said, "yes", with excitement because I trusted him – I believed it wasn't going to hurt. So, I stretched my little leg out in front of me, (shoe was cute, too) and put my foot out there, the other kids huddled around to watch. He pointed and positioned the BB gun in a downward position aiming towards my right foot, but he pressed the BB gun into the top of my foot and fired full blast. My foot was in immediate great pain and my face flushed red. Crying loudly, I quickly removed my shoe and saw that the cuneiform (top of my foot) was

blistered red. I was crying everywhere. He could have blown my foot off. I don't know where my foster parents were or what happened next, but I survived. All guns are dangerous.

July 4th Celebration: Old Lady Next Door

At the age of eleven years old, on the 4th of July— at almost sunset, our neighbor, a mean elderly African American woman who wore a short curly black synthetic wig, a black knee-high dress, and thick black framed, bi-focal eye glasses – she came outside yelling and screaming at me while waving and pointing her black hand gun at me. She was standing on her door steps, peeking from behind her door screen – threatening to "blow" my "brains out" because I placed my packaged fireworks on her car trunk to use as a table as I prepared to lite them and throw them in the streets to celebrate Independence Day. I quickly grabbed my fireworks, ducked and dodged and ran across the street where two African American men stood watching the scene unfold as I hid between two parked sedan cars in fear of my life that she was going shoot me in my back. That crazy old woman scared me away; I was scared to death. She went back inside her house and slammed her door.

Alarmingly, *"firearm injuries are the leading cause of mortality among children and adolescents 1-19 years old in the USA." Furthermore, children ages "15 years old or younger unintentionally killed themselves or another child. Children "10-14 age group, 32.3 percent of shooters were a friend of the victim." (Authors: Arti Vaishnav, Gary A. Smith, Jaahnavi Badeti, Nicole L. Michaels, [https://pubmed.ncbi.nlm.nih.gov/37357309/]).*

Forehead Injury

 During the Christmas holidays, in the fourth grade I suffered a severe head injury at school which left me with deep facial scarring on my forehead and consequently, affected my brain development. I was rushed to Oakland's Children's hospital on a stretched gurney with a gash in my forehead, bloody face – knees were damaged and numb. I could barely see and walk. The Christmas lights and everyone around me were blurry; I don't remember faces – only their voices and physical presence. While in the elevator on the gurney, I overheard the doctor give the nurse strict instructions to keep me awake as they prepared me for an emergency surgery or I could die in my sleep. I remember the bright lights in the surgery-room, the doctor who was very gentle, the needles in my forehead, the stitches and the nurses in white clothes around the surgical table. According to my foster care records, my social worker reported my head injury to my aunt and grandmother. I vividly remember my foster mother arriving at the school around the same time as the ambulance who then rushed me to the hospital.

Molestation

 Another day, still in the same foster home, I was about eleven years old – same neighborhood, several doors down from our house, one day after school – just a normal day; my babysitter who was my foster mom's neighbor, her husband tried to rape me! My foster mother instructed me to always go to our neighbor's house in the event she wasn't home after I walked home from school. So, this particular school day – I did, I went to my babysitter's house and it turned out disastrous! I walked up a short flight of stairs, knocked on the front door and the babysitter let me in her house. She was nice and politely instructed me to sit in the living-room with her husband who was already watching television and that she would be in the backyard with the gardener. There I was alone with her husband, whom I did not know. I was tired and my back pack was heavy, so I said "hi" to her husband – he said "hello." He appeared to be in his late seventies or early eighties. He wore a dark shirt with dark, cotton or polyester pants and had a black walking cane leaning against his lounge chair.

I sat down on the love seat (which had plastic covering, popular in the 1970s) adjacent to his lounge chair that he sat slouchy in — slightly three feet across from him. He was about six feet tall, dark skinned, half bald with big black framed, bi-focal glasses. I could see his eyes very clearly and up close. He looked creepy, like the mean old African American lady down the street. He kept staring at me after I sat on the couch. Suddenly, he straightened up his poster and sat up. Then, he kept staring at me. I looked at him. He would look away and watch TV. But, next time, he kept staring at me. I would stare back because I was beginning to be uncomfortable being alone with him. He was pretending that he was watching TV, but then he began to touch his private parts — his genitals — in front of me. He quickly unzipped his pants and pulled out his dark shriveled genitals, then momentarily covered it with his hands - looked at the TV — then looked at me again, but this time he pointed to his genitals covered with his left hand. My fear level at this point was heightened. I was in shock and frozen, I didn't know how to respond to his perverted acts, yet. But, I remember, I fiercely tightened up and prepared to jet out the living-room at any moment if he attempted to touch me. I couldn't believe this old dude. We had an intense brief stare down. It was going to be me or him. He broke off the stare down, and anxiously, with his right hand, reached in his back pocket to get his wallet uncovering and fully exposing his naked genitals, which looked like a black old dead snake waiting to be buried. I was still in shock and scared to move, but I watched his every move very closely as I eased closer to the left side of the love seat — a quick exit to the kitchen. He then opened his wallet and anxiously shuffled through his cash bills.

Unbeknownst to him, I was fully aware of what was taking place and mentally preparing myself to get the heck out of the living-room without him attacking me. Suddenly, he reached towards me with the cash that my feet quickly turned into fireball feet. I jumped off the love seat and yelled and screamed as loud as I could as I ran towards the kitchen and back yard where his wife and gardener were. He was up out of his chair right behind me, but he quickly and sneakily sat back down in his chair because he heard his wife rushing up the back door stairs. She opened the door frantically, looked at me and asked what was happening. But I was still trying to get out the back door to get to safety and far away from her perverted husband. She grabbed me tightly by my shoulders and asked "What baby?!" "What?!" "What's going on?!" She looked at me, then looked at her husband "What is going on?!" I explained to her what her husband had done. She angrily and quickly confronted him — he denied the accusations and rolled his eyes at both of us while continuing to watch TV. She rushed away from him towards me and said "baby he's old — he is an old man" "don't you worry about him." She yelled at him again and told him to stay away from me and gave me strict instructions to stay with her in the kitchen until my foster mother and sibling arrived to take me home. When my foster mother and sibling arrived, the babysitter and my foster mother both got into a heated verbal argument — I was never sent back to that house again. I don't remember the police ever being called and neither was it reported to my social worker.

I am not shocked that *"Youth in foster care represent a highly traumatized population." And, a "likelihood of lifetime PTSD diagnosis are associated with this specific trauma. Additionally, "the highest probability of lifetime of PTSD diagnosis were rape, being tortured or a victim of terrorists, and molestation." (Authors: Salazar AM, Keller TE, Gowen LK, Courtney ME. Trauma exposure and PTSD among older adolescents in foster care. Soc Psychiatry, Psychiatry Epidemiol. 2013 Apr;48(4):545-51. doi: 10.1007/s00127-012-0563-0. Epub 2012 Aug 17. PMID: 22898825; PMCID: PMC4114143.)*

Foster Home Transfer

Sometime after my head injury and babysitter incident, I demanded to be placed in new foster home because I didn't feel safe there anymore. A few days later and after a verbal argument with my foster mother, my social worker picked me up and dropped me off at Snedigar Cottage (a government holding facility in Alameda County for foster youth). While waiting to be placed in a new foster home, I was almost raped by a sixteen- or seventeen-year-old African American male teenager. During the incident, thank God I was able to fight him off and scream loud enough that a Caucasian female corrections officer came running around the hallway corner and confronted the evil teen about his intensions for attempting to force me into an interview room with intensions to sexually assault me.

As I was walking into the main office building and he was leaving, he noticed me and suddenly grabbed me and tried to lock me in the interview room with him. He covered my mouth, grabbed my arms, and shirt but I fought him off and screamed loudly. He denied the accusations and the corrections officer told him to hurry and get back to the male side of the facility.

Somehow, back then, in the late 1970s, preteen boys and girls under the age of 18 would share common areas or path ways to access the main office which had long unattended hallways that led to the front office window. The common areas were unsupervised hallways and out-door areas such as the outdoor foyer in front of the main building which led to the main office. Children in the Snedigar Cottage facility was not escorted to the front office by corrections officers, we walked alone leaving from inside the main holding facility, down a long flight of concrete stairs leading to the main office – which had an allure of easy access to kidnap children or an escape for potential runaways.

Snedigar Cottage had an open-door runaway policy that allowed teens to leave without notifying anyone in the building. When I first arrived a young African American girl my age, about eleven or twelve years old, we were sitting down in general population, talking for a few minutes about leaving the facility but I wasn't serious – I didn't want to run-away; the conversation led her to ask me to "run" with her and to hitchhike our way around town until we could find a place to go. I said "no" – I declined her invitation because, 1), I didn't know her well, I just met her, and 2) I remembered the rapist "Stinky" who my mother told me was a wanted serial rapist in the Bay Area. I also knew it was unsafe to get into cars with strangers. A few days later she had run-away from the facility, I never saw her again.

Our rooms looked like jail cells. The metal doors were blue and opened electronically. Our cell was furnished with one stainless steel toilet, a stainless-steel sink, blue lockers, two metal beds with blue body length polyester cushions and pillows for the top and bottom bunks. Girls showered two or three at a time in front of female corrections officers who handed us dry towels after showering. My stay there was for only three weeks. After I was placed in my new foster home, I saw the same guy who tried to rape me – he was at the playground when I was out playing with other children. I was sitting on a swing talking and playing with neighborhood friends in a small park adjacent to Webster Elementary School. I sensed a stranger staring at me from afar, whom was a young African American man sitting in the park's parking lot with other adult men. He looked at me with a snaring evil-eye, that's when I realized he was the bad guy at Snedigar Cottage. I left the park and went home because I was fearful of being in the presence of this evil guy.

Birthday Fail

"Hey dirt!" This is another strange but dangerous incident that happened to me while in my new foster home. The sun was shining brightly – it was my twelfth birthday and my new foster mother gave me money to pay for and watch a movie cinema at the Eastmont Mall in Oakland. We lived right across the street from Webster Elementary where I attended school as a fifth grader. When I left home headed to the mall, my hair was styled in a cute afro-puff and I was wearing a pretty knee-high print dress, with long white transparent socks pulled up to my knees and white tennis shoes.

My walk from home through the neighborhood was nice, the trees were green, no loose dogs, etc. not much loitering, but a few people here and there. Nothing stood out of the ordinary until I reached the main cross street (can't remember name) from East 14th. I remember feeling safe walking alone, although I wished someone had walked to the movie theater with me because the farther I was away from home while walking, the more I began to feel afraid of being alone. But technically I was not alone because of adjacent neighborhoods and the afternoon automobile traffic.

So, I was about half-way to the mall and I reached the main street of two-way traffic. I decided to cross over to the other side because the Eastmont Mall was on the left side of the street. As soon as I crossed the street, I saw a bus stop on the corner with a light skinned mixed race

African American male teenager standing behind it on a low hill of poorly landscaped grass. There was a little pink house right behind him. I made it across the street safely and immediately, the teenage boy engaged me with the words: "Hey dirt!" "Gimmie yo' money, dirt!" I stopped briefly to look at him but continued walking as I ignored his mean assertions of me as "dirt," because he looked disturbingly, creepy.

He confused me momentarily because I was clean as a whistle and he was dirty. He was filthy wearing dirty khaki-colored pants, a dirty jacket, dirty face, a dirty dark colored cotton beanie and underneath was his light brown curly hair seeping from sides, and he was holding a wooden stick in his hand as though he was king of the jungle. Maybe, he was homeless or something, I didn't know or care at the time but he looked like no one cared about him. A dirty mean teenage bully, about 14-15 years old.

He could see that I had stuffed my birthday money in my socks. As I got closer to the bus stop, gradually, he proceeded to walk down from the grass hill closer to me, yelling and saying "Hey dirt!" "Gimmie yo' money!" At this point, I realized he was going to rob me or do something bad to me. I was scared! But I was bold enough to say "no!" and began walking faster to get farther from him – but he began to chase me. My feet and adrenaline went into full gear. I hit the concrete running like a track star – never looking back, right into the middle of oncoming traffic on East 14th street. I was so afraid for my life; I ran into the street without looking before crossing. I was in the middle of the street having a stop-n-go life or death situation. Cars were suddenly slowed or at full stops and honking their car horns as I struggled to safely get across the street.

Because once I realized I was in the middle of the street, I saw all these cars quickly approaching me. I froze for a moment to figure out how to safely get out of the two-way traffic – didn't know if I should run back or go across the street because I didn't want to get hit by oncoming traffic and I didn't want the bully to catch me. But finally, I was able to safely get to the other side of East 14th – near the traffic light. When I looked back – the bully was gone. My socks were rolled down to my ankles – my birthday money had disappeared. The money fell out of my socks while I was running from the street bully. This was a bittersweet unfulfilled birthday – I felt really sad because I could have been seriously injured or killed but by the grace of God, I safely survived that incident. Picked up my sad face and I walked into the Eastmont Mall to call my foster mother from a pay phone booth. I explained to her what happened – she quickly drove to the mall and picked me up and we went home. I never saw the street bully again. He probably bought a hamburger and fries with my money. Soap would have been a better option for him though, because he was filthy.

Hungry Latch-key Kid

In retrospect, intermittently when my sibling and I weren't in foster homes and living in the cities of Oakland and Berkeley, California, between of the ages of nine and twelve, I remember living as a latch-key child. My siblings and I were left home alone often with no food or supervision, all the time, and at times with no electricity. We were hungry, without food all day on some weekdays and weekends. In an old brown house, we lived off East 14th street in east

Oakland, adjacent to an empty parking lot (weed lot.) Most days, I would walk through the weed lot where the African American male drug dealers would loiter in the parking lot where I would watch them sell drugs, daily. They would chat and laugh with each other, drink beer and whiskey, and sit in their Eldorados, Cadillacs and hoopties until they exhausted their day or until sunset.

Towards the end of the evening or early in the mornings when the weed lot was empty, I would search through the broken beer bottle glass on the ground and dry weeds growing up from the concrete for dropped twenty-dollar bills or whatever I could find. Most days, I would find nothing. On some occasions, I would find money to buy a little food to eat or cigarettes for my aunt, because back then a pack of cigarettes only cost twenty-five to seventy-five cents.

Then, while living in Berkeley near San Pablo Avenue, we rarely had food in the house when my mother was gone – as a result, in the mid-afternoon, we would leave home, break into school cafeterias and recreational centers during after school hours or weekends and steal graham crackers, fruit and apple juices or go to the corner store or closest grocery store to steal food for a snack or dinner. Or, we would sneak into our neighbor's backyard down the street with our clear mason jars and pick the blackberries from the vine against the fence. Once the mason jars were filled, we would go home, mix water and sugar with our blackberries, then smash them with our spoons, eat them and enjoy a warm afternoon of fresh fruit.

On other occasions, during the day, we would walk down San Pablo Avenue and gather trash from the ground (anything that looked valuable – scraps) and put them in a raggedy small box, stand on the sidewalk and attempt to sell worthless stuff to strangers walking by. If we could sell something for a nickel, dime or a quarter, it could buy us some candy. No one would ever buy our trash. As a further solution to our hunger, I began to steal my next-door neighbors Coca-Cola bottles from their front porch, each day, and cash them in for food or candy. They were worth about ten cents a bottle in the late 1970s. I continued to do so until one day the Coca-Cola bottles disappeared, they stopped showing up. At that age in my life then, I didn't know I could work for food, if I could, I would have. I was just a hungry street kid. A year later, at age eleven, back into foster homes, which I already shared, I eventually got my first job as a newspaper girl which was a fun cool experience. I didn't have to steal my food anymore and my new foster parents cooked full meals every day. But, eventually, after being transferred to another foster home, and living with relatives, when my mother returned home, at age thirteen, I was medically diagnosed as "malnutritioned" because my body was undernourished.

And, I don't know what happened to "Beauty" with the bony rib cage, she was the starving neighborhood dog at the brown house, off East 14th – a Black stray mut who would wonder through our neighborhood for food. Dried dog poop on the grass was her meal when strangers didn't feed her.

On My Own

As I mentioned earlier, I was a single parent in high school. When I finally left home with my baby boy at the age of nineteen, I didn't have a high school diploma and didn't complete my GED until three years later. I was the monarch butterfly with all the different colors who finally left her cocoon to find my own path. Often, I felt like my life was in different colors because the colors reflected different phases or moods in my life or the environment I lived in at that time. I can identify with the monarch butterfly – with her growing process, because it has to crawl as a caterpillar before it can fly.

So, there I was, the world was mine. This street kid who was now a young African American woman with a baby boy attempting to build a nest of my own and I had no idea how I was going to bring home the food. In contrast, as the process of my young adult life began to unfold, I remember feeling like I survived a thunderstorm. I was on my own – a young adult mother who finally had an opportunity to carve my own path in the world. But little did I know, I was walking into a dark room only to look for the light switch. There was no light for years.

"In 2021, 21.6 per 1000 African American teen mothers, ages 15-19, gave birth in the United States." (California Dept. of Public Health, Birth Statistical Master Files [March 2020]; CDC WONDER, Nationality, California Dept. of Finance, Population Estimates and Projections [June 2023], www.kidsdata.org, a program of Population Reference Bureau).

While still pushing through and searching for my first apartment, my only solution to avoid homelessness was to accept free housing from a local African American woman referred to me by a childhood friend who said the woman had an extra bedroom I could use. We met; she was nice and made me feel welcome. But, after briefly settling into her home, I didn't notice right away because she was private but friendly and clean– she had an addiction to crack cocaine. I watched her tweek, steal from people and sell her personal belongings for a hit only to fall deeper in poverty and damage her brain cells. She was sixteen years older than me and explained that she was fired from her job (a large corporation) where she worked for 20 years and fallen into a deep depression. During one night, I had awakened to warm my son's bottle of milk, walking from my bedroom though the hallway to the kitchen and noticed the apartment had a sweet and sour smokey smell. The woman was laying on her back on the couch while holding a mid-size mirror watching herself get high off crack cocaine. I was afraid to complain

about the smell because she was providing short-term temporary housing and a free room. But I did ask her why did she "get high using the mirror"? and she said, she didn't want to "burn her lips." Soon, I noticed this was an ongoing behavior so I moved out of her apartment immediately to stay with out-of-town relatives. She lost everything – became a crack cocaine corner addict and one day found dead of a crack cocaine overdose. Before she died, I'd always wondered if she had gotten better but I was informed her crack addiction led her to the street corners. I went looking for her and found her standing on the corner, mid-day, with strange African American men. Their bodies were malnutritioned from the weight loss effects of crack cocaine and they had badly blemished skin and worn dirty clothes. Her hair was dirty and uncombed – she greeted me with a smile, unashamed and said, "Hi Felicia," with a stern look in her eyes that said "don't judge me" and she immediately began to beg for money. But I was still shocked by the condition of her whole self, her body – she explained that she was doing okay out there (holding her sweater tightly around her body). Her physiological decline was apparent, so I didn't complain about her request for money neither pry in her personal business – I gave her a few dollars immediately because I had compassion for her circumstance. At a point in my life, she had compassion for me when I had no home to go as a young single parent. When I walked away with these images of her outside on the corner like that, I deeply wondered would she ever get better. I never saw her again; rest in peace, sis.

According to my research, some African American women addicted to crack cocaine had *"Treatment readiness barriers". They "lacked motivation for treatment (personal), the belief that treatment was not needed (personal) and the obstacle of interpersonal relationships with family and childcare (interpersonal reasons). For personal barriers women often delayed or avoided treatment because they changed their mind, wanted to manage their own, or had problems making arrangements." (Author: Department of Preventive Medicine and Public Health, University of Kansas School of Medicine-Wichita, Wichita, KS Corresponding Author: Michelle L. Redmond, Ph.D., M.S., Department of Preventive Medicine and Public Health, University of Kansas School of Medicine-Wichita, Wichita, KS 67214 https://www.ncbi.nlm.nih.gov/pmc/articles/PMC7032990/).*

After I burned that bridge, my relatives provided temporary housing until I could find employment, enroll in adult education and college classes, and get my first apartment. My life was inching forward but I still felt empty as my mind was always thirsty while attempting to conquer this big world with an infant boy child.

Within a span of five years as a young adult mother, I met more and more Black women who were single parents, too. Some were my age or much older, single or dating but unmarried and in physically abusive romantic relationships with men who were dangerous to their household. Children were dying to gun violence in and out of the home. Other women were struggling to maintain reliable housing, steady employment and successful entrepreneurship while others had brief stints in county jails and prison for theft, fraud, prostitution, drug convictions and drug addictions.

In 2022, there were approximately *"4.15 million African American family households with single mothers in the United States". "This was an increase from the 1990 levels, when there were about 3.4 million Black families with a single mother". (Published by Veera Korhonen, https://www.statista.com/statistics/205106/number-of-black-families-with-a-female-householder-in-the-us/).*

My previous statement is not to say there were no Black women working in stable careers or successfully thriving. The silent women in this story are those who became lawyers, doctors, nurses, teachers, cooks, cosmetologists, counselors, bankers, athletes and many other occupations in high demand throughout America.

Life Revelation

Finally, I was getting closer to finding that light switch that I couldn't find in the dark earlier. I found it — I had an epiphany. It showed me that any time there's a group of people who have not been given strong long-term structure for their lives and no vision for their future, you will find a collapsed community of people who began to fall into

invisible cracks. Some of those cracks are small, some are large — and people get stuck in them. So, I began to distance myself from anything or anyone who was a distraction and didn't want to see the best of me emerge. Slowly I began to scrape, exist and survive while creating a life of nowhere. Life had thrown me the curve ball — The Bittler Black Curse.

I went after my forty acres and a mule — the Afro American dream with this Bitter Black Curse in my shadows. In combination with my childhood traumas, young adulthood traumas, America's built-in discriminatory housing, employment and educational systems were causing my future to collapse. I prayed, trusted, worked, went to school, sweated, long-suffered, and loved — worked my butt off. I birthed two beautiful children, married my high school sweetheart, and waited for everything to fall in its rightful place while scraping for everything my family and I needed. Too much of my future was being controlled by outside influences. There was no warning — just WHAM! That quick. The symptoms of the Bitter Black Curse had attacked my heart, self-esteem and my livelihood. My life had become symptomatic — I was broken and left for dead with severe emotional pain, a broken heart, unforgiveness, uncertainty, hopelessness, agony, shame and years of the shock of chronic deadly stress.

In fact, an example of chronic stress is PTSD (post-traumatic stress) "Black women experience a disproportionate burden of PTSD and chronic stressors in middle age such as problems caused by family members, health, disability, work, financial poverty, law enforcement and discrimination. Experiences of discrimination contribute to neurobiological changes in emotion regulation adding to the severity of PTSD. When present, PTSD among Black Americans is often chronic, severe and goes untreated." (Authors: 1. Informatics, Decision-Enhancement and Analytic Sciences Center (IDEAS), Veteran Affairs Salt Lake City Health Care System, Salt Lake City, UT 84148, USA; 2.Department of Internal Medicine, School of Medicine, University of Utah, Salt Lake City, UT 84132, USA; 3.Program for Research on Black Americans, Institute of Social

Research, Ann Arbor, MI 48106, USA; 4.University of Michigan, School of Social Work 1080 S. University Ave. Ann Arbor, MI 48109, USA; 5.Departments of Epidemiology and Statistics, Fielding School of Public Health, University of California, Los Angeles, CA 90095, USA; 6.UCLA Center for Bridging Research Innovation, Training and Education for Minority Health Disparities Solutions (BRITE), Los Angeles, CA 90095, USA; 7.Department of Psychology, The New School for Social Research, New York, NY 10003; 8.Departments of Psychology and Health Policy and Management, Fielding School of Public Health, University of California, Los Angeles, CA 90095, USA. https://www.ncbi.nlm.nih.gov/pmc/articles/PMC9175561/).

In retrospect, there are warnings of chronic stressors because the human body senses things – stuff: it can see, feel, hear, smell and taste (five of our natural senses). And, some of those warnings can cause instantaneous pain or a build-up of pain which is not immediately recognized. For instance: the human body is designed like a house; the skin is its paint and inside the house is a lot of stuff – things humans put inside the house or at times the house is already furnished – with stuff. The house was built with a roof, a wooden frame and paint to weather the storms just like the human body. The human skin was meant to weather most storms with additional added shelter such as clothes. But the human eye can detect what kind of storm the outside of your house (your body) has weathered because the paint begins to peel, the roof begins to sag, the wooden frame is deteriorating – the house looks weak – the human body looks weak. The inside of the house has cracked paint in the walls – we feel the pain but we ignore it. The dry paint has cracks that hasn't had a new layer of fresh paint in years.

Most times, the human body can hide what's going on inside the house, but we can't hide what's happening outside of the house. People see us. We see each other surviving and existing while walking over the cracks that shadow each step we take. It follows us throughout our lives. The warning signs are always there ready to be repaired but somehow our human bodies ignore the problem until it's too late. Like the human body, a house has a voice. When it speaks, with leaky roofs and peeling paint, people can see and hear that something is wrong. The symptoms are always there. The Bitter Black Curse makes it difficult for the human soul to survive.

God had not forsaken me; he did not forget me and I was tired of being shut off from a place of mindful peace. Early one afternoon, I looked in the mirror and I looked at the stone-cold walls in my mind one last time. I knew that my mind, spirit and my heart were still wounded but I was finally able to remove some of the metaphorical bandages and stitches.

Here's another example of how The Bitter Black Curse metaphorically works throughout the

The dark tone surrounding the cracked concrete symbolizes the Bitter Black Curse (the pressures of life), a dark spirit which causes the concrete to crack – like the dry skin of the human body or the neurological cells in the brain and human nervous system. The crack in the concrete follows human beings around our entire lives because of the pressures caused by the pains of life- The Bitter Black Curse.

human life span. The photo above is a picture of cracked concrete used to demonstrate what happens the moment a human being is born – we are broken. At the beginning of birth, human beings become broken by evil sinful spirits that travel through other human beings which immediately, and consequently affect our livelihood and future the moment we are born into the world. During the middle of the human lifespan, after years of tolerated pressure, the cracks become larger causing more pain. And, towards the end of the human lifespan, the human body collapses (see above picture) because it can no longer tolerate the pressures from The Bitter Black Curse.

The solution to conquering the Bitter Black Curse is to live by faith and not by sight. Human beings are going to suffer. We harm ourselves out of ignorance and others hurt us because of their own ignorance's and suffering, too. The crack in the concrete as demonstrated above is going to damage us; but the key is not to focus on the crack but focus on your faith – your future. Your faith becomes the light needed to see past the dark spirit of The Bitter Black Curse. You must have faith so you don't ever become the Wandering Black Woman suffering from the Bitter Black Curse.

If you are her – begin to trust and believe in yourself. It's not easy. It takes time and sincere everyday effort to cope and heal. Quick example – I'm not suggesting that anyone does this literally: Imagine there's a ten-flight of stairs nearby with rocky steps and smooth steps to go from the first floor to the tenth floor in a tall corporate building with no elevators – no easy way up. To get to the top of the building you must take the first step to reach the second-floor level. After reaching the top of the second-floor level, repeat the same steps of sincere effort to reach the top of the third, fourth, fifth, sixth, seventh, eighth, ninth and tenth floor.

The further you get to the top of the staircase (your divine calling) of any building or place (purpose in life) the farther away you can pull yourself out of the cracked concrete and out of the gloom of The Bitter Black Curse. This step is essential to the next stage of transforming your life.

Reach for Your Crown

After accepting that you have suffered from The Bitter Black Curse and you're no longer the Wandering Black Woman, prepare to reach for your crown – the [moral] crown – the crown you were born with – your birthright - your new journey, your future. A crown can be for a woman or a man, but in this instance, I'm specifically speaking about women. This process is technical and smoother to help pinpoint what is going on in your life and what is needed to keep moving forward on a positive healthy path progressively.

My childhood and young adulthood traumas in life as I have demonstrated will differ from other women of color of course, however; if you believe that you have suffered from the Bitter Black Curse, or are suffering because someone or something has seriously altered your livelihood or on the edge of a mental health crisis, get help immediately. Talk to a medical professional, a counselor, a minister, whatever is good and will work for your personal situation to push through to cope and heal.

Emerge. Whatever effects The Bitter Black Curse has had on you and is now under your control, it's time to emerge and evolve – emergence. To come into view. To emerge is the process of coming into the light (a vision in your mind). Coming into sight – to reveal (to see and touch physical things, to see and understand the world [people, places and things] in its actual existence.) Emerging is the actualization– to be seen out of secrecy and privacy. For instance, imagine that you've always desired to create your own designer perfume. First step – prepare yourself emotionally and psychologically to confidently do the work as the concept was imagined in your mind. Second step: emerge, read a book to teach you how to create the perfume (*the first two steps are the process of your thoughts emerging out of your mind into actual existence*), third step – get started – after you've read the book, create the perfume or accomplish the activity or goal you have wished to achieve.

Moving progressively. I created the Felice Bois Theory Grid© on the next page to help women accomplish goals by analyzing their life-situations, then applying the strategies in the theory grid to help overcome constant barriers that interfere with personal achievements. It's not a total solution to adversity, but an individual can make mental notes by remembering selective contents of the theory grid or by manually taking notes and apply the theoretical strategies to common and prevalent life situations.

The Felice Bois Theory Grid© can be used by individuals who are ages twelve and older, can read, write and comprehend. It can be used independently for individuals to help transform from one lifestyle to a new lifestyle, can be used in groups or teams, by high school students, college students, entrepreneurs, job seekers, hobbyist or parents structuring a lifestyle for children to achieve short-term and long-term goals while working towards accomplishment within their life journey. Each individual applies the Felice Bois Theory Grid© strategies to their individual reality or life situations.

The illustration helps 1) to provide a visual recall of the information 2) help organize and structure short-term life situations when common prevalent interferences cause set-backs such as money management, obtaining adequate housing, moving to a new state, seeking employment or starting a new family. Individual goals will vary person to person. This theory grid is not a final solution to everyday problems or life situations, so I encourage women to use as many resources that are applicable to their personal life situation.

Inspiration and Motivation

On another note, individuals resistant to necessary healthy adjustments, in addition to having a bad attitude, those individuals will have difficulty pursuing a progressive life journey. This kind of behavior builds a propensity of laziness and a lifestyle of transiency – causing someone to just exist and except whatever cards are dealt to them. So, make sure while pursuing your crown, that you are working towards something that truly inspires and motivates you and prepares a sincere desire to achieve your goals – short-term or long-term. Sometimes, just getting out of the bed is an excellent start.

Inspiration, motivation, mental and physical transformation requires necessary adjustments to achieve a heathier more rewarding human experience.

Therefore, the efforts put into understanding and applying the usefulness of The Felice Bois Theory Grid© can help most individuals reach the goals they are seeking if the individual can embrace a new attitude with a positive approach to achieve the goal. However, it is a limited resource and its use is not recommended for emergency or life-threatening situations.

The Felice Bois Theory Grid©

Stages A, B, C, D = (Four stages of fundamental life situations)

Stage (A) Life Situation	Stage (B) Life Situation	Stage (C) Life Situation	Stage (D) Life Situation
Emerge; Get started	Neutrality	Evolved	Incline/Decline

- **Life –** "The quality that distinguishes a vital and functional being from a dead body; the sequence of physical and mental experiences that make up the existence of an individual; one or more aspects of the process of living". ~*merriam-webster.com/dictionary*

- **Situation –** "The way in which something is placed in relation to its surroundings; state of health, position or place of employment; position in life; position with respect to conditions and circumstances; relative position or combination of circumstances at a certain moment; a critical, trying, or unusual state of affairs; problem; a particular or striking complex of affairs at a stage in the action of a narrative or drama". ~*merriam-webster.com/dictionary*

- **Real-life –** "If something happens in real life, it actually happens and is not just a story or in someone's imagination". ~*Collinsdictionary.com*

- **Stage –** "A period or step in a process, activity, or development: such as the growth of the human body". ~*merriam-webster.com/dictionary*

- **De-stressor –** To release bodily or mental tension; unwind; get rid of feelings of stress. ~*Cambridge.org; merriam-webster.com/dictionary*

DISCLAIMER: The Felice Bois Theory Grid© is not intended to replace legal or medical assistance in a real-life emergency. Call 911 or contact your local authorities during a real-life emergency.

The Process of Fundamental Life Situations

Stage (A) – Emerge; Get Started: This is the phase when an individual conceptualizes an idea or plan with the intent to start a specific activity; a short or long-term goal which the individual desires an end result of success or achievement. Discipline, persistence, patience, resilience and a de-stressor is suggested.

Stage (B) – Neutrality (strategize the plan to obtain the goal): After the individual has emerged and started their activity in Stage (A), neutrality is the phase to develop and meditate on a strategy to grow and complete the activity or reach a specific individual goal. Not recommended to become neutral and idle. An individual must always strategize to push through day-to-day interferences to reach for and remain in Stage (C). Discipline, persistence, patience, resilience and a de-stressor is suggested.

Stage (C) – Evolved: This is the phase when an individual has accomplished their activity, short or long-term goal(s) in Stage (A) and Stage (B) where the individual has emerged, strategized, developed and has gradually grown and matured. Discipline, consistency, patience, resilience and a de-stressor is suggested.

Stage (D) – Incline/Decline: **The Incline**: This is the survival phase to maintain consistency in the usefulness of the accomplished activity or goal which were accomplished through the processes of Stages (A) emerged, (B) developed and strategized and (C) evolved, which resulted in an incline of the accomplished activity or goal. More importantly, individuals who reach the incline of Stage (D) will experience an esteemed confidence and achieve higher goals. **The Decline**: Day-to-day life interruptions/multiple life situations and personal barriers can temporarily place an individual back in Stages (A) or (B) depending on the life situation. Discipline, consistency, patience, resilience and a de-stressor is suggested.

The Felice Bois Theory Grid© Part 2

The Seven Elements a Life Journey Must Include in a Vision

The "vision" comes out of the human heart (*the spirit of the person; mental images that project a future desired accomplishment*) and the "vision" creates and is the desired mission within the life journey. The life journey exists because the vision has been revealed and should include the following foundational elements: **1)** A Purpose   **2)** Direction **3)** Inspiration **4)** Motivation **5)** Transparency **6)** Integrity **7)** Mental Flexibility.

What is the purpose for your life journey? What direction is your life journey taking you? What is your inspiration and motivation for your life journey? Does your life journey reflect the integrity of your moral principles? Change brings conflict. Throughout your life journey, the inevitable highs and lows of multiple life situations requires a life-long resilience of mental flexibility from the beginning of Stage (A), in the middle of Stages (B) and (C) and during Stage (D) – the incline and decline within your life journey. Be prepared to adjust to the demands of any life situation.

Illustrations of Group Processes in Stages (A), (B), (C)

(Individuals of two or more in each group)

Group 1: Individuals "Get started" (Stage A), in "Neutrality" (Stage B) they overcome conflict quickly and achieve their goals or success at a faster pace evolving and staying consistent in Stages (C) and (D).

Group 2: Individuals "Get started", (Stage A), in "Neutrality" (Stage B) they struggle with conflict, strategizing, developing and growing – take a little longer to succeed but they overcome and reach their goals evolving to Stages (C) and (D).

Group 3: Individuals "Get started" (Stage A), but they get stuck in "Neutrality" (Stage B) with strategizing, developing and growing due to life interferences or personal barriers. They have time lapses of days, months or years before these individuals eventually mature and evolve to Stages (C) and (D).

Group 4: Individuals "Get started" (Stage A) but they never strategize, develop or grow. This group of individuals usually have too many barriers and obstacles to overcome, are not determined or motivated to move to Stages (B), (C) or (D).

The Significance of De-stressors

De-stressors are important life tools to strengthen the mental and physical well-being of an individual and are needed to prevent an individual from suppressing mental and physical pain; and to survive life-situations of Stages (A) through Stage (D). As soon as an individual is relieved by the use of a de-stressor(s), the individual can start over, bounce back stronger, be better and re-focused.

Stressors – Mental and Physical	**De-stressors** Choose De-stressors Applicable to Your Lifestyle
Fear, anger, doubt, discouragement, frustration, emotional or physical abuse, other types of physical pain, psychiatric melt-down (*anxiety, depression, etc.*), addictions, family, marital or employment problems.	Rest, relax, cry, prayer, church, exercise, music (CDs, online streaming or live), quiet-time (alone), eat healthy foods, counseling, romance (kiss/hug), reading and writing (Audio storytelling, novels, write poetry), watch positive TV, get fresh-air.

Life Goals and Multiple Life Situations

An individual can have one life goal with multiple life situations effecting its progress. For example: The Felice Bois Theory Grid© provides a visual illustration to help organize an individual's thought process by merging fundamental life situations of Stages (A) through (D) with expected and unexpected multiple life situations to achieve the individual's life goals. But life situations are unique to each individual's circumstance. An individual may have to surrender (accept what cannot be changed) to life situations of hardships to excel through Stages (A-D).

Your journey is about trusting your heart. Your heart is the vision that God put in your mind to move from start to finish. But everything must be completed in the middle to get to your final destination. The middle is the most difficult trying times and having some structure with clarification, helps your life situations process (flow smoothly) easier. Here's a quick illustration:

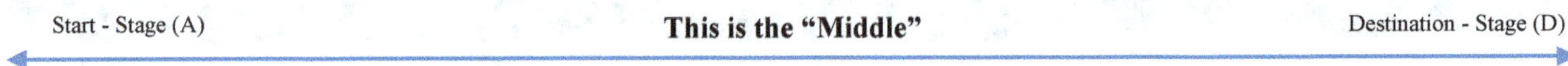

The "Middle" is where everything happens while on the life journey.
Do everything necessary to work through your life situations to accomplish your goals – reach your destination – your future crown.

It's okay to have life goals with multiple life situations; most importantly, understand how to access the resources needed to survive once your journey has begun and manifested. And, guard your vision (your heart) because it determines the course of the rest of your life.

Under the correct authority and in the right mind, any woman can get control and transform her life and start reaching for her crown. Women come from all walks of life throughout the world, so if at some point in your life, you've felt lost, don't lose yourself again while wandering, existing and surviving and living aimlessly. All women must learn to embrace who they are now to embrace her future for tomorrow. Get your crown as often as you have earned it.

SIDE NOTE: Write an Action Plan to organize your strategy, then execute your Action Plan into practical use so that it's no longer an idea but an effective manifested reality. An Action Plan includes a series of steps to accomplish your goal. Re-strategize and reorganize your Action Plan as needed until your goal is accomplished.

What Every Black Woman Should Never Become

The Bitter Black Witch

While reaching for the crown – your future, there's going to be moments when you see other women succeeding financially and spiritually in life – those are excellent attributes for any woman – however, here's the truth about two types of women who are succeeding in the world today, they are women as described in Stage (A) and Group 1 of the Felice Bois Theory Grid© - they emerge, get started and quickly evolve becoming successful in most of these categories as: God fearing women, cooks, educators, fitness experts, healthcare providers, attorneys, beauticians, engineers, scientists, truck drivers, financial planners, dancers; they're family oriented or a mix of all of them. They are not perfect women, but they've made life work for them against the odds. They were determined, they work harder than average women – they evolved quickly and have rightfully earned their crown, or 2) they lie, cheat, seduce and steal – they do whatever it takes to reach their golden crown of success – with no apologies intended and no life in financial or material poverty. These women are both good and bad women. Yes – they are both good people who succeed and bad people who succeed. And, regardless of how their success was obtained, they're not going to stop because you're not there yet, or because their success bothers you.

When you see or meet women as I have described, don't get jealous and envious because they strategized, developed, matured and evolved into the success they desired for their lives, no matter their career choice – even if they lied, cheated or seduced to get to the top. These are women with practical human desires *(they are getting paid, some have created families while learning to balance love and romance, they have beautiful houses, clothes, nice cars; others are leaders in their communities, they have occupational and vocational certifications or licenses, college degrees, etc., and a good sense of street smarts – they transform with the times).*

Don't hate on other women who work hard to create a lifestyle to support and enrich their lives while you sit on the wall like a wall flower who evolves into The Bitter Black Witch – watching another woman's every move and doing nothing or struggling to obtain your own personal success.

Indolence – laziness; that's what happens to women who haven't accomplished much or outright jealous women who are haters and focus too much on the success of other women, thus, leaving the hater – The Bitter Black Witch, too distracted to use her own mind, her hands, fingers, her arms, legs, feet, her heart – her whole body – everything God blessed her with to become better – to be part of something meaningful or greater and worthy of living for within her own self.

The Bitter Black Witch lacks fortitude – she doesn't have the courage or resilience to endure through adversity without hurting others. So, while reaching for your crown, you have to reposition yourself from slothfulness or indolence to emerge to Stage (A) and strategize your plan in Stage (B), then graduate to Stage (C) and (D) to reach for and maintain your future goal – to reach your crown. You have to tap into all your senses and natural gifts and make your own money even if you haven't identified those gifts or natural human elements yet, get to moving to find out what's inside you – not what occupies the other woman.

Looking back, conquering The Bitter Black Curse as well, can leave emotional and financial setback scars leaving some women to feel unsuccessful, undesirable and unmotivated to work through their life situations. So, whichever path you have chosen to achieve your future crown, don't get stuck in Group 4 – women who get stuck in Group 4 become The Bitter Black Witches, they never make good progress –or good life choices – they always regress – they make no life improvements and get left behind. She is either a woman who has fallen from the grace of being a successful woman or a woman who lacks integrity, a trouble-maker – she is a "zero" – she is nothing and adds no true value to the existence of the human race, her life, her family or others around her.

The Bitter Black Witch exist in age groups of girls who are in their early adolescent years, ages ten to nineteen, and adult women in their twenties, thirties, forties, fifties, sixties, seventies and older. Bitter Black Witches are heartless "thirsty" evil women of any social status (*prestige*), social group (*educational accomplishments*) and any ethnicity. They are cold, unfriendly, selfish, abusive, vicious, godless, desperate, envious, hateful, jealous and walking dead women. They need psychiatric and emotional help. They project a complex superiority over others, criticize other women unfairly, belittle them, create rumors with an attempt to destroy the livelihood of other women who they secretly desire to emulate or the pure evil in the spirit of The Bitter Black Witch desires to harm other women without provocation; they watch, plot and wait.

But, The Bitter Black Witch – she too, with a sincere desire, can heal (with help), emerge, grow, mature out of her darkness into a beautiful transformation and become a light of inspiration – a greater value to her community and to those in her immediate circle.

If you sense the spirit of The Bitter Black Witch creeping in your ear – run, run far, far, far away from it. Use your de-stressors (see Felice Bois Theory Grid©) to fight her off with everything you got. Or, if you meet a woman who carries the spirit of The Bitter Black Witch – help her, if at all possible, be kind regardless of her behavior or avoid her when possible. Unless she becomes a Stage (A) woman, she'll never understand the vast wealth of wisdom that you carry in your spirit and she could potentially become envious and dangerous to your future crown. If at all possible, never let The Bitter Black Witch control anything connected to your future crown.

If reaching for your crown seems difficult you might need to re-strategize and give yourself or the life situation, you're struggling with time to subside or develop and mature more. Stay focused on your mind, body and spirit as they emerge, develop and evolve. Your gift and talents will lead you to the success that is purposed for your life. Let the accomplishments and support of other resilient women inspire you to work harder to achieve your life goals.

Victim of Brain-Picking

It is inevitable that a woman will need help along her life journey. She will meet new people and for one reason or the other, people from her past will resurface. As your life is moving forward day-to-day, don't become a victim of brain-picking. A brain-picker can be a woman or man from any ethnicity. Brain-pickers are selfish, charismatic, influential, insecure manipulating bullies – unashamed. They are abusive (*physically or mentally*) and enjoy an unreasonable amount of physical and emotional control over other individuals.

Brain-picking is when someone allows another person to psychologically pick their life apart to re-define and control an individual's life according to the brain-picker's terms (ideas, or concepts) and values. It's a form of "gas lighting", or mind-control through cult indoctrination or brain-washing to sneakily persuade gullible individuals to follow and become like them, subsequently, and eventually convincing their victims they are worthless without them. Their specific goal is to gain access to information the victim has, with the brain-picker's intentions to build rapport, a friendship or romantic intimacy to emotionally and psychologically control the victim. The most common things a brain-picker is seeking is money, sex, affection, or material things. Their victims are usually successful, everyday working people; women with children, young women, the elderly, disabled, homeless, and individuals with low self-esteem; these individuals are usually faced with difficult life situations and are in desperate need for help.

Brain-pickers are good at criticizing and using repetitive negative words to mentally distort the self-image of the victim, and by giving false narratives of their victims to others. This type of manipulation creates a cloud of control over the victim because the brain-picker is controlling how outsiders mentally see the victim and how the victim sees themselves. A cloud of control keeps others at a distance causing outsiders to only see the brain-picker's narrative of the victim. Keeping outsiders at a great distance gives the brain-picker more control over the victim's self-image.

"Self-image is perceived internally causing introspection (observation of one's own mental and emotional process; thoughts and feelings" – *[merriam-webster.com and Dictionary.com]*). This perception examines an individual's entire human existence while creating a mental image of a self-concept based on the values and beliefs that an individual believes about themselves resulting in an outward projection of one's self to others. Throughout this entire process, the victim must control their whole mind, if not, the brain-picker will control the other half of their mind creating internal mental confusion that distorts their self-image causing unnecessary multiple life situational interferences, embarrassment and long-term emotional and psychological scars.

Most importantly, don't emulate a brain-picker and don't become one. In other words, an outsider or anyone looking [in], should not control the self-image of any individual.

Cult-Culture of Whoreism

This is one of those moments when you push back them baby hairs, take off your lace-top, remove your synthetic braids, your eye lashes, earrings, make-up and acrylic nails – so you can see.

We've seen them in our neighborhoods and on television – pimps and whores. They've been around since the beginning of time. In today's society, it's popular to be a pimp and

a whore – they make a lot of money. These are two or more people who have formed a partnership to make money by selling sex. When we see them, they look gritty, and they smell like seduction – pretty waxy cosmetics, cheap perfume, the cigarette smoke or a joint – (the blunt). Some are high paid pimps and whores and others are street, cheap, low paid pimps and whores.

The dynamics of pimping and whoring has a striking appeal of power, survival, danger, greed, lust, sex, money and drugs – that seductive combination alone is enough to destroy the human race, literally. We don't even need nuclear bombs – pimping and whoring [is] a nuclear bomb because humans are destructive, which is another sad reason literal nuclear bombs exists – because of the greed of power, the need to survive, seduction, the allure and control of sex, money and drugs – whoreism. Humans will do anything to control everything because it gives humans a sense of superiority – a god-like power.

What is a cult-culture of whoreism? It is systemic demonic worship – systems of prostitution *(people, places or things characterized as being prostituted for monetary gain),* the satanic spiritual mother of all whores – The Great Whore; a sex cult, defiled people, controlled by the same mind, filled with lust, controls people with unclean spirits – male and female. It's an obsession with lust – lust works its way through seduction which then creates channels for more demonic spirits to access their desire of recreational sex with strangers who are liars, thieves, adulterers, pedophiles, rapist, and murderers. The love of sex, money, drugs, and material possessions has created lies and emotionally dramatic behaviors in people controlled by the spirit of whoreism. The beliefs and values of some racial, political and other social groups are the biggest influential factors in this type of cultural dominance which is the doctrine of whoreism – it is their god.

The doctrine of whoreism is a powerful and seductive doctrine – it has complete mind control over its cult (group of people), in essence, the group of people lose authority and control over their everyday thoughts, therefore, losing independent decision making in any moment. Most people don't realize they live in a culture of whoreism because they unseeingly were taught to live sexually explicit lifestyles. They either love the life of whoreism, trapped in it, or have not learned an alternative more rewarding lifestyle.

Keep Your Legs Closed: The most popular forms of whoreism are women and men who live their lives as whores ("hoes"), prostitutes, hookers, pimps, madams, street hustlers or other high-profile sexually explicit images of women to elicit a response for monetary gain, or unwanted responses from onlookers. Some single unmarried women and men take on forms of whoreism by practicing sexually promiscuous lifestyles for sexual recreational pleasure with strange multiple sex partners – some individuals, believing that it's an expression of love.

It's normal to desire affection from people – it's also normal to want to be held, to be hugged and kissed, to show and receive affection, but whoreism is far from love – it is not love and my guess is about fifty percent of women who have lovers deceptively believe that their lovers love them – they don't – they love the sex – the lust and excitement that whoreism brings. This type of delusion happens to women and men seeking love from strangers whom have never had a companion to love them. The other fifty percent of women and men usually catch on to the scheme of their lustful behavior of whoreism, and dissolve the "bad girl" or "bad boy" self-image they created for themselves as being "easy." Because, anybody can have an "easy" body because their bodies belong to anybody – anybody is whoever the "bad girl" or "bad boy" has a strong lust filled physical attraction to and presumes the prospective lover can bring them sexual stimuli and consequently, experiencing a false sense of love.

Whoreism Is The "Great Whore" In the World: A whore can be male or female, but "The Great Whore" is a woman [it] has many filthy faces. Anybody can have the "Great Whore." It belongs to anyone who opens the door to its clutches: the greed for power, sex, money and drugs the obsession over these things is controlled by the "Great Whore" and belongs to the "Great Whore" and anybody is subjected to the seduction of the "Great Whore." And, in hindsight, the psychological and emotional damage – the atrocities done to people throughout the world, the "Great Whore" is going to be destroyed, because the "Great Whore's" light [darkness] destroys lives.

Whoreism Is A Camouflage of Love: (*a mix of evil and emotional intense seduction*) opposite of the instinctive kindness and good will of others. It has created streams of lust filled with seduction through acts of pedophilia, homosexuality, pornography, rapist, sex trafficking, infidelity in marriages, leading to unwanted pregnancies, baby daddy and mama dramatics, sexually transmitted diseases, severe mental illnesses, suicides, drug addictions, alcoholism, parents who murder their children, mass incarcerations and godless sick empty people. All of these issues have permeated throughout the earth, into our homes, communities, our churches, schools, legal systems, including the politics that governs our nations.

Guard the Five Human Senses: And, furthermore, guard your senses of eye sight, sound in the ears, smell of the nose, taste of the mouth and touch of the skin – not to avoid living in an environment in the presence of people, but to keep the most important five senses of the human body closely grounded when they are triggered for a response. I'm not insinuating that an individual be stiff necked or act as though the five senses of the human body have no effect on our daily lives – that wouldn't be normal. In fact, it is through "free will" that God has allowed human beings to experience the full immersion of those five senses within the human body. My point is this – the pure reality and the allure in whoreism is not only deceptive but it's deeply rooted and controlled by the misrepresentation of the five senses in the human body, contrary to Gods original design which allowed humans to connect within the world around us – to other people, animals, places and things without being judged or be controlled by the lust of the human body. But, we're human, Adam and Eve happened, life happened – this is where we are and how humans have developed throughout history, in all racial cultures, including the Black culture, worldwide.

Whoreism Destroys the Prospects of Healthy Romantic Relationships: As I mentioned previously, in the "Keep Your Legs Closed" section – whoreism is a powerful seductive scheme that capitalizes off the loneliness of promiscuous individuals – especially single Black women. Women who ignore this fact are engulfed with sexual lust filled desires that controls every fiber in their existence. They won't get it yet, but they will potentially or they will continue to create an "easy" path for manipulative men who are not their husbands to creep in and lay-up with them for purposes of simple and free sexual entertainment.

This type of single woman does not belong to any specific single man – and the man she is currently laying up with – her sexual partner, "her man," neither does he belong to any specific woman. And the main reason these two individuals, in this instance, are not married is because they don't really know each other yet, they are not friends and they don't know that they will never love each other – not yet.

However clever the deception – the continuous response to the control and seduction, sexual relationships like this might imply that the sexual relationship is about love, but it's not. Relationships like these can begin innocent but evolve into fantasy and entertainment. Subsequently, when the word "commitment" joins the relationship – this is a human element that completely throws off sexual relationships because only one person will truly commit – most likely will be the woman – and possibly, neither the woman or the man will commit, leading up to consequences that will negatively impact the rest of their lives. Because the outward appearance of couples who are seen by others as a couple, may appear to their friends and family as monogamous but these types of relationships usually end up broken off due to sexual and emotional affairs with other people outside the sexual relationship – new entanglements. Unexpected pregnancies, new baby daddy and baby mama drama, child support check schemes and the "I hate you!" "I never loved you!" "You cheated on me!" or "You never believed in me, anyway!" Yelling and bickering back and forth, name calling, bullying – verbally and or physically abusing each other and never ending the sexual relationship.

Consequently, violent sexual relationships like these quickly fester into sex cults because couples with narcissistic behaviors won't allow them to break off intense "going nowhere" love-hate sexual relationships – with no genuine commitment or responsibility for each other but to maintain the sexual fantasy and emotional control. They cheat on each other – the woman has multiple sex partners and the man has multiple sex partners creating a crazed cult of women fighting over the man and men fighting over the woman. None of them belong to each other – none of them are married to each other – they don't love each other – they want to control each other – they are afraid of being alone and becoming better and they won't commit to a monogamous meaningful spiritual marriage – consequently, the damaged sexual relationship is left "as is," resulting in the stereotypical system of sexual fornication.

A man does not belong to the woman until the sacred ring of "I do" is on the wife's ring finger and throughout the duration of the marriage; the wife's body belongs to the husband exclusively and the husband's body belongs exclusively to his wife: (*"The wife has no power of her own body, but the husband; and like-wise also the husband hath not power of his own body, but the wife,"* 1 Corinthians 7:4, KJV).

The allure of physical attraction, good sex, fast money, drugs, good food, extended family and entertainment can hold up a sexual relationship for a short time to over a span of years but the relationship will never be morally whole because neither the man or the woman has learned to sacrifice individually to produce [better versions] of themselves [first] or to earn the love and respect they desire from each other; consequently failing the relationship and blocking a prospective love interests who is probably a more suitable and sincere companion anyway.

Women are who controlled and lost in sexually lustful behaviors must make God her number one friend on this earth. He will show her things no man can. Not her boyfriend, her daddy, her brother – none of her well-known friends – it is God. I respect ambitious women who work hard –have alluring side hustles to earn money to pay bills – to survive – but why allow her mind, body and spirit – her value – be limited to only sex, especially if the sex is free. Think about it – a woman's only real personal value is her vagina? Her sex? And, it's free?! No. Of course not. And, I'm not referring to women who have been sex trafficked, because that is forced sex labor - a separate entity of systemic whoreism. However the act of sex is pursued or received, a woman's body was made for more than sex, more than just a commodity to appease strangers – in contrast, the human body was created to be respected as the temple of God, which is a much-needed discipline to be practiced more often in every culture and not restricted only to Black women but to all men and women: *("Do you not know that you are the temple of God and that the Spirit of God dwells in you?" 1 Corinthians 3:16-17, KJV).*

Solving A Cult-Culture of Systemic Whoreism: Using a practical approach, to set a higher standard of personal living, it begins with making personal sacrifices. To stop the unwanted lustful or sexual behavior, identify the specific lustful impulsive desire(s), or cultural behavior(s), in honesty, that's causing the specific whoreism which is negatively impacting an individual's life or a group of people lives. Replace the negative behavior *(the sacrifice – giving up the negative behavior that's not good for the individual or group of people)* with correction, something positive to encourage and manifest positive and healthier desired results. However, this practical sense of correction may not be sufficient for all individuals, because *human will-power (self-control)* cannot maintain this type of resistance permanently.

Second, lust and sex some-how, control the outcome of many things, however dominant the force and desire of the lust or sex, it is the responsibility of people to understand the doctrine of that specific control – in this instance – it is the doctrine of systemic whoreism.

In the case of systemic whoreism, the spirit of this cult is controlling, evil, sneaky and has taken something sacred, such as sex, and contaminated the purity of sex – which was created and originally reserved for the marriage of a man and a woman. But, in all practicality, it is common for most individuals to have pre-marital sex, this behavior is practiced worldwide, in every culture and every race of people. Consequently, we [people] give this behavior permission to potentially create emotional and physical harms in the lives of married people, children, and single adults searching for love or any individual desiring sexual entertainment.

Going back to personal sacrifices, there is also spiritual relief – or spiritual perspective. In combination with applying practical approaches, the most effective relief from systemic whoreism is to find the "water," a woman has to be thirsty for life in the Gospel of Jesus Christ – Jesus Christ is the "water," who gives new life (John 4:10-14, KJV - *"But whosoever drinketh of the water that I shall give him shall never thirst; but the water that I shall give him shall be in him a well of water springing up into everlasting life").*

It is the act of repentance (sacrificing or steering away from a sinful nature) and public baptism that cleanses the spirit, (Acts 2:38, KJV), (1 John 1:9, KJV), therefore, allowing an individual to control, eliminate whoreism and have authority over a renewed and spiritually cleansed mind. It's not about having religion to free people who are trapped in whoreism, it's about believing and practicing the truth that Jesus Christ taught people so they [we] can be free in mind, body (the flesh) and spirit giving an individual control over unwanted and excessive lustful desires that lead to a false sense of power, false sense of being a deity [God/Goddess/God Like] behaviors, disappointing and disastrous lifestyles. This level of liberation can only be obtained through constant repentance and prayer – through Jesus Christ who is the son of God: *("I am the way and the truth and the life: no one comes to the Father except through me," John 14:6, NIV).* There are people who don't believe in God, and that's their prerogative, however, the *will-power* of any individual will always be tested, even for people who have had the *will-power* to walk away from the lifestyle of whoreism – these are anti-god or non-believing people.

What athiest, non-believers and gnostic individuals don't have is consistency in the *will of God* because they don't know God. What they have is: *will-worship* – a mind of carnality *(natural state of the human mind, separate from God– sinful nature),* believing the human body can accomplish anything by the *will-worship* and not by God the divine. And, because the *will-power (self-control)* of human beings run dry without spiritual conviction of the Holy Spirit, which means, without an "escape" from "temptation" of a conceived lustful unwise desire, the human flesh obeys the *human will (capacity to decide)* when the *will of God (Spirit of God)* is not present (Romans 8:7, NIV; 1 Corinthians 10:13, NIV). If there is no conviction, then after an individual's threshold of *will-power* has exceeded what it can physiologically bear, then lustful desires repeatedly begin to control the mind, body (the flesh) and spirit of an individual. Consistent behavior in resistance – the discipline of prayer and repentance, and staying away

from people, places or things that will lead an individual back into the control of whoreism.

Outward adornment is secondary to inward beauty because inward beauty is everything that's beautiful inside a woman's heart – so when expressing one's self outwardly by the wearing of fashionable attire, it's okay to wear beautiful clothes, with beautiful hairstyles or to wear make-up and beautiful jewelry – of course, each style of outward expressions is tailored to the woman's personal beliefs and values because not all women wear make-up and jewelry. In particular – just have consciousness, awareness and perception of your mind, body and spirit when presenting it to others privately, at home or in public. Because, when a woman isn't conscious of her intentions while wearing and expressing herself through outward adornment, other people begin to attach unsolicited sex (whoreism) to the woman's self-image if the woman's body is appealing or "sexy" due to the shape of her body or the type of clothes worn, the style of her make-up, hairstyles, jewelry, her shoes and even the way a woman walks and speaks can be misconstrued as something else – just be yourself and grow from there.

Defining Modern Day Black Momma® is not about avoiding the pain and struggles of being a

Black woman, it is about overcoming the struggles that pain caused and finding the strength to reach for the [moral] crown. The crown holds a woman's past, her future and everything else a woman achieves or inherits – her pain and accomplishments – the crown is the woman's birthright – her purpose (small and big/unnoticed and publicly recognized) – the Queen's chair – her empire.

A woman doesn't have to inherit an empire or kingdom nation on earth to be a Queen – the empire is already given at birth. To sit in the Queen's chair, four things must happen: The woman must: 1) Acknowledge her [moral] crown, 2) Accept her crown 3) Wear her crown daily, 4) Walk in her life purpose (*this is her empire*) – the rest will follow. So, during a woman's lifespan, the [moral] crown she wears slowly matures into acceptance (being a Black woman and/or a mother), responsibility and Gods wisdom (not of her own).

All women are crowned at birth – we were born to accomplish a purpose worthy to benefit the livelihood of people from all cultural backgrounds – even people from afar – the poor, the rich, the blessed, unblessed, sad, unhappy people and the unreachable.

A woman's crown is a personal honorary distinction – a reward of completion and of accomplishment while living on earth. Thinking about it…traditionally, the crown belongs at the top of the woman's head for a reason – the [moral] crown she was born with before the tangible, jeweled, golden and silver crowns existed – women were born with our own crowns:

the [vision] and/or purpose or revelation God gives a woman for her life. The vision embodies the mind, body and soul of the woman.

And, as demonstrated throughout Black History in the 1960s and 1970s for instance, the Women's Rights Movement was a perfect example of women who used their moral crowns to fight for our civil rights, legal rights, equal rights and diverse equal opportunities to: eat, sit, worship and live wherever we chose; to explore educational and career opportunities worthy of equal pay, to be included in local and world politics – to vote for our own rights – permission to be free from bondage of our past and present conditions that have unnecessarily trapped women of color with bad relationships or places within their communities that destroy a prospective flourishing future.

Most women of color aren't aware of what we can do with the crown we were born with because [human nature] is so powerful, so oppressive, that the plague of pains in life deprived so many women of color the divine [vision (revelation)] God had given them – [us], individually at birth.

That's why it's important to push through, because as Black women, in the African Diaspora, we must understand who we are first *(identifying, understanding and accepting the past)*, who we are now *(how have we evolved?)* and be honest with ourselves when we look in the mirror each day. Who is she, anyway? Whoever she is, she must not get stuck in the stereotypical self-image of the *Wandering Black Woman (she has her crown but she doesn't see it, yet)*, *The Bitter Black Curse* or *The Bitter Black Witch* roaming in this world – in America, Latin America, the Caribbean Islands, Great Britain or any other part of the world women of color may exist.

I know we have lost many lives of Black women due to so many socioeconomic harms such as the atrocity of slavery, community safety issues, discrimination in housing, employment, education and a lack of financial resources. Severe mental health issues – suicides, criminal acts of homicides and drug addictions all have affected our communities, not to mention, the physiological strength of the family dynamics, and our hope for a better commonality. But for those Black women who still stand, breathe, walk, live, and thrive with a greater determination and seek a deeper connection within themselves, that's who this book is for, those women who are pushing through to higher and rewarding grounds.

Take God with You on Your Journey: Forgive yourself first. Then forgive those who somehow, with an authority out of your control hindered your life and swept you under the rug with an attempt to derail your life – throw you off track. Even if it's from a distance, forgive your enemies to remove their weight of darkness from your life. God gave us the power of forgiveness to retain as much control as possible over our minds, our lives, our hearts and our future. People who attempt to sway you from taking God with you on your life journey are not your real friends – they are your enemy. Because in secret, they desire to know the same God you are taught to avoid because the sovereign God and his son Jesus Christ have the real answers to solve our everyday problems we face while reaching for our crowns on this earth – Proverbs 3:5, ESV, Proverbs 3:6, ESV.

Why I Believe in God: God is everywhere – he is omnipresent – in the invisible and physical. Everything in this earth derived from the breath of God - I believe in the "creation" as explained in the book of Genesis. God is the etymology of the existence of the universe, the heavens, outer space, the sky, the human race, the earth and everything that exist in it. During my youthful years, I've always believed in the existence of God, but I was not holy neither was I whole. At some point in life, individually or collectively, people must acknowledge the existence of God. People worldwide cry out for help to God instinctively because our spirits are inclined to reach for the truth beyond what mankind can provide. It is God who breathed life into the human soul, not a scientist – into the soul of your parent's and your ancestors. The spirit of God lives in every human being and in every living creature on earth.

Don't Get Lost in Social Circles: Imagine living and floating around in outer space in the troposphere, stratosphere, mesosphere, thermosphere and exosphere – the human body wouldn't survive – it would freeze to death or burn wandering in the outer space. That's how some women live today. Wandering around from one place to the other and tagging along with whomever will tag her back. Have fun, but don't get lost in social circles that derail your goals and get you off track from your purpose and life journey.

Own Your Freedom: Shaping the meaning of a Black woman's life though her self-image and her self-esteem is essential to every Black woman's success in this world, so remember to recognize and embrace the stage of life you are in now and to be progressive and not regressive because we are free women and not in physical bondage. Black women are beautiful Black people born to be free and not to be dominated by physical or mental societal chains, but to be the women and mothers we were meant to be; free to have unbiased life experiences that bring us joy and free to tell our true stories to inspire and motivate others. We have a human right to have a healthy, committed, purpose-driven direction for our lives without being disregarded as insignificant in the earth. Subsequently, even more essential to every little Black girl throughout the world because her first role model is the Black woman. And, it is through our ancestry, DNA lineage, our family lifestyles, our soul food, religion, politics, fashion, our kinky coily hair and brown skins tones – our Black culture, that we will forever be the Black woman – The Modern Day Black Momma® reaching for her crown.

Seek Medical Assistance: If you are experiencing a suicide or mental health medical emergency, please contact a trusted friend or relative, local clinic or hospital to speak with a licensed medical professional.

Take good care of yourselves ladies! Remember to reach for your crown every day.

Felice Bois

P.S., thank you for reading my self-love essay!

FOLLOW ME ON SOCIAL MEDIA

Share Your Experience on Social Media: If you enjoyed reading this self-love essay, please share your experience on social media using #moderndayblackmomma.

My Website: Moderndayblackmomma.com

Mdbm.tv

Twitter.com/Felicebois

Reverbnation.com/Felicebois

Youtube.com/@TheRealFeliceBois

Facebook.com/Moderndayblackmomma

Facebook.com/MDBMrecords

Instagram.com/Felice.bois

Tiktok.com/Diamond.blackoil

Amazon Music: Search for "Felice Bois" or "MDBM TV™, The Real Felice Bois

Spotify PODCAST: Search for "Felice Bois" in Podcast Category or type this URL into a web browser: https://tinyurl.com/MDBM-TV-Podcast

Spotify MUSIC: Search for "Felice Bois" or type this URL into a web browser: https://tinyurl.com/Felice-Bois-Music

Other Products

Gen Eyes Wide

Acapella Spoken Word

Digital download available for $18.99 at:

www.ModernDayBlackMomma.com

Enjoy listening to transformational, acapella spoken word storytelling? Consider purchasing the seventeen-track classic, 2009 digital CD album, Gen Eyes Wide, featuring popular motivational songs in acapella spoken word: Modern Day Black Momma®, Angel of Yo' Own War, Laborer and the Street Hustler, Brown Skin, Who You Gone Be, Lock Down Den, Neva See, Prayer fo' You, Heaven on the Run and a host of other inspirational songs on the album to enjoy.